ANOKA COUNTY LIBRARY
707 COUNTY ROAD 10 N.E.
BLAINE, MN 55434-2398

READING GROUP CHOICES
2022

Selections for lively discussions

Reading Group Choices' goal is to join with publishers, bookstores, libraries, trade associations, and authors to develop resources to enhance the shared reading group experience. *Reading Group Choices* is distributed annually to bookstores, libraries, and directly to book groups. Titles included in the current and previous issues are posted on ReadingGroupChoices.com. Books presented here have been recommended by book group members, librarians, booksellers, literary agents, publicists, authors, and publishers. All submissions are then reviewed to ensure the discussibility of each title. Once a title is approved for inclusion, publishers are asked to underwrite production costs so that copies of *Reading Group Choices* can be distributed for a minimal charge. For additional copies, you can place an order through our online store, contact us, or contact your local library or bookstore. For more information, please visit our website at **ReadingGroupChoices.com**.

Cover art, *Too Hot to Sleep* by Jenny Kroik (2021)
Design by Sarah Jane Boecher

Copyright © 2021 Reading Group Choices LLC

All Rights Reserved.

Published in the United States by Reading Group Choices LLC

ISBN 9781733268349

For further information, contact:
Reading Group Choices
info@ReadingGroupChoices.com
ReadingGroupChoices.com

PRAISE FOR *READING GROUP CHOICES*

"We have learned over the years that displays are a great way to encourage circulation at our small, rural library. One of our best displays is based on the wonderful literary guide published by Reading Group Choices! ... Patrons cannot wait to get their copies and start reading. We sincerely LOVE your product and feel that it helps us create one of our favorite displays EVER."
—**Gail Nartker, Sandusky District Library**

"Reading Group Choices continues to be a first-rate guide for those delicious reads that book group members enjoy reading, and that prompt the most enriching discussions." —**Donna Paz Kaufman, Paz & Associates, The Bookstore Training Group**

"I recommend Reading Group Choices as the number one starting point for book clubs. The newsletter is fantastic, and I especially like the Spotlight Book Club section. It is a nice way to meet other book clubs. I am very happy with the book selections offered by Reading Group Choices. Thank you for this excellent service." —**Ana Martin, Cover to Cover Book Club, Hollywood, FL**

"Not only is Reading Group Choices a great resource for individual readers and book groups, it's also an invaluable tool for teachers looking to introduce new books into their curriculum. Reading Group Choices is a brilliant concept, well executed." —**Kathleen Rourke, Executive Director of Educational Sales and Marketing, Candlewick Press**

"I love your book, website and the newsletters! As an organizer of two book clubs, it's so great to get an early line on upcoming titles. The hardest part is waiting so long to read the book! By using recommendations from your newsletters, I can build a list of monthly book selections one whole year in advance." —**Marcia, CCSI Book Club**

"Quail Ridge Books has worked with Reading Group Choices for many years and the guide has been sought out at our twice yearly Book Club Bash. The prize bags of books have been a highlight. We are great partners in getting good books into the hands of people who love to read and discuss books."
—**René Martin, Events Coordinator, Quail Ridge Books**

Welcome to
READING GROUP CHOICES

"As you read a book word by word and page by page, you participate in its creation, just as a cellist playing a Bach suite participates, note by note, in the creation, the coming-to-be, the existence, of the music. And, as you read and re-read, the book of course participates in the creation of you, your thoughts and feelings, the size and temper of your soul."

—**Ursula K. Le Guin**

Dear Readers,

Welcome to the 28th edition of Reading Group Choices!

The past year has again been challenging for book groups, but we are inspired by the creative ways in which groups have continued to connect, read, and meet.

We have watched groups transition to virtual and outdoor meetings. Many groups have created new traditions they are going to continue such as meeting in outdoor parks and going for walks while they discuss books. It is wonderful to see how transferrable books and discussion can be. You have proven that discussions can happen anywhere and anytime. And we are so pleased we can continue to offer new recommendations and resources for such creative fellow readers and book lovers.

The new edition includes a variety of fiction, nonfiction, and young adult titles from a range of authors. We hope these titles will inspire many thoughtful, interesting, and important discussions. Some books are available now and some will be available in 2022 so you can plan ahead.

There are longer versions of the conversation starters available online in our searchable database, along with author interviews and excerpts. Be sure to sign up for our eNewsletter, where you can find out about new monthly recommendations and giveaways as well as other resources for your groups.

To order more copies of this edition or past editions, visit our store online at www.ReadingGroupChoices.com.

We hope you enjoy another year of discovering, sharing, and reading new favorite books, and continuing the conversation through all modes of discussion!

M.M.

Mary Morgan
Reading Group Choices

Contents

FICTION

All the Little Hopes, Leah Weiss *12*

Black Buck, Mateo Askaripour *14*

The Book of Otto and Liam, Paul Griner *16*

Her Here, Amanda Dennis *18*

The House of Rust, Khadija Abdalla Bajaber *20*

In the Face of the Sun, Denny S. Bryce *22*

The Jane Austen Society, Natalie Jenner *24*

Leave the World Behind, Rumaan Alam *26*

Libertie, Kaitlyn Greenidge *28*

Little Foxes Took Up Matches, Katya Kazbek *30*

The Movement, Petra Hůlová *32*

The Mysteries, Marisa Silver *34*

The Mystery of Mrs. Christie, Marie Benedict *36*

Nightbitch, Rachel Yoder *38*

Noopiming: The Cure for White Ladies,
Leanne Betasamosake Simpson *40*

Olga Dies Dreaming, Xochitl Gonzalez *42*

The Phone Booth at the Edge of the World, Laura Imai Messina *44*

Reeling, Sarah Stonich *46*

The Saints of Swallow Hill, Donna Everhart *48*

The Second Life of Mirielle West, Amanda Skenandore *50*

The Second Mrs. Astor, Shana Abé *52*

Small Things Like These, Claire Keegan *54*

The Spanish Daughter, Lorena Hughes *56*

This is Happiness, Niall Williams *58*

Three Sisters, Heather Morris *60*

The Trees, Percival Everett *62*

The Vanished Days, Susanna Kearsley *64*

The Very Nice Box, Eve Gleichman & Laura Blackett *66*

Walking on Cowrie Shells, Nana Nkweti *68*

The War Nurse, Tracey Enerson Wood *70*

Waterfall, Mary Casanova *72*

NONFICTION

Dancing with the Octopus: A Memoir of a Crime, Debora Harding . . *76*

Footnotes: The Black Artists Who Rewrote the Rules of the Great White Way, Caseen Gaines *78*

Gichigami Hearts: Stories and Histories from Misaabekong, Linda LeGarde Grover *80*

The Kissing Bug: A True Story of a Family, an Insect, and a Nation's Neglect of a Deadly Disease, Daisy Hernández *82*

A Matter of Death and Life, Irvin D. Yalom & Marilyn Yalom *84*

October Child, Linda Boström Knausgård *86*

Pastels and Pedophiles: Inside the Mind of QAnon, Mia Bloom & Sophia Moskalenko *88*

Remember: The Science of Memory and the Art of Forgetting, Lisa Genova *90*

This Time Next Year We'll Be Laughing: A Memoir, Jacqueline Winspear *92*

Three Ordinary Girls: The Remarkable Story of Three Dutch Teenagers Who Became Spies, Saboteurs, Nazi Assassins—and WWII Heroes, Tim Brady *94*

Watershed: Attending to Body and Earth in Distress, Ranae Lenor Hanson *96*

YOUNG ADULT

The Black Friend: On Being a Better White Person, Frederick Joseph..*100*

Diary of a Young Naturalist, Dara McAnulty *102*

Indivisible, Daniel Aleman *104*

Mad, Bad & Dangerous to Know, Samira Ahmed *106*

Maybe We're Electric, Val Emmich *108*

The Nature of Witches, Rachel Griffin *110*

Nothing Burns as Bright as You, Ashley Woodfolk...............*112*

Passport, Sophia Glock *114*

Strong as Fire, Fierce as Flame, Supriya Kelkar..................*116*

We Are Not Broken, George M. Johnson *118*

FICTION

ALL THE LITTLE HOPES
Leah Weiss

A Southern story of friendship forged by books and bees, when the timeless troubles of growing up meet the murky shadows of World War II.

Deep in the tobacco land of North Carolina, nothing's been the same since the boys shipped off to war and worry took their place. Thirteen-year-old Lucy Brown is precocious and itching for adventure. Then Allie Bert Tucker wanders into town, an outcast with a puzzling past, and Lucy figures the two of them can solve any curious crime they find—just like her hero, Nancy Drew.

Their chance comes when a man goes missing, a woman stops speaking, and an eccentric gives the girls a mystery to solve that takes them beyond the ordinary. Their quiet town, seasoned with honeybees and sweet tea, becomes home to a Nazi prisoner-of-war camp. More men go missing. And together, the girls embark on a journey to discover if we ever really know who the enemy is.

"Weiss's magic turns the local into the universal." —**Wiley Cash**, *New York Times* bestselling author of *A Land More Kind than Home* and *When Ghosts Come Home*

"Wrapped in hope and mystery, this beautifully crafted story … is full of heart." —**Kathleen Grissom**, *New York Times* bestselling author of *The Kitchen House* and *Glory Over Everything*

"Leah Weiss confirms the place she's earned among top-notch historical fiction writers." —**David Gillham**, *New York Times* bestselling author of *City of Women and Annalies*

ABOUT THE AUTHOR: **Leah Weiss** is a Southern writer born in North Carolina and raised in the foothills of Virginia. Her debut novel *If the Creek Don't Rise* was released in August of 2017. Her short stories have been published in *The Simple Life* magazine, *Every Day Fiction* and *Deep South Magazine*.

July 2021 | Paperback | $16.99 | 9781728232744 | Sourcebooks Landmark

CONVERSATION STARTERS

1. Lucy's mother points out that language is meant to communicate, not separate, which discourages Lucy from overusing her enormous vocabulary. Throughout the book, how do you see language used to communicate? To separate?

2. Describe the role of the Browns in their community. What are the broad effects of being a bibliophile?

3. What do you think about the mystery of Trula Freed? Was her magic plausible? Have you ever had an experience with a spiritualist or medium?

4. Lucy and Bert argue about treating Nancy Drew like a real person. Can you think of any literary characters that you wish were real or who felt as real to you?

5. Though purple honey in North Carolina is rare but real, what role does it play in the book? Did it arrive just to cure the mysterious flu, or is it a symbol for something larger?

6. Describe the relationship between the Riverton community and the German POWs. What effect does Terrell Stucky have on the reputation of the POWs? How do the Germans come to be an accepted part of the town?

7. During her father's funeral, Bert realizes how much she's changed since she left home. Do you agree with her sister that she doesn't belong to the mountains anymore? How is "home" defined throughout the book?

8. What do you think comes next for Lucy and Bert and the rest of the Brown family? How do you think their experiences and decisions will affect their futures?

BLACK BUCK
Mateo Askaripour

A *New York Times* Bestseller

A Read with Jenna Today Show Book Club Pick

For fans of *Sorry to Bother You* and *The Wolf of Wall Street*—a crackling, satirical debut novel about a young man given a shot at stardom as the lone Black salesman at a mysterious, cult-like, and wildly successful startup where nothing is as it seems.

There's nothing like a Black salesman on a mission. An unambitious twenty-two-year-old, Darren lives in a Bed-Stuy brownstone with his mother, who wants nothing more than to see him live up to his potential as the valedictorian of Bronx Science. But Darren is content working at Starbucks in the lobby of a Midtown office building, hanging out with his girlfriend, Soraya, and eating his mother's home-cooked meals. All that changes when a chance encounter with Rhett Daniels, the silver-tongued CEO of Sumwun, NYC's hottest tech startup, results in an exclusive invitation for Darren to join an elite sales team on the thirty-sixth floor.

After enduring a "hell week" of training, Darren, the only Black person in the company, reimagines himself as "Buck," a ruthless salesman unrecognizable to his friends and family. But when things turn tragic at home and Buck feels he's hit rock bottom, he begins to hatch a plan to help young people of color infiltrate America's sales force, setting off a chain of events that forever changes the game.

Black Buck is a hilarious, razor-sharp skewering of America's workforce; it is a propulsive, crackling debut that explores ambition and race, and makes way for a necessary new vision of the American dream.

"Askaripour closes the deal on the first page of this mesmerizing novel, executing a high wire act full of verve and dark, comic energy." —**Colson Whitehead, author of** *The Nickel Boys*

ABOUT THE AUTHOR: **Mateo Askaripour** was a 2018 Rhode Island Writers Colony writer-in-residence, and his writing has appeared in *Lit Hub, Catapult, The Rumpus, Medium*, and elsewhere. He lives in Brooklyn, and his favorite pastimes include bingeing music videos and movie trailers, drinking yerba mate, and dancing in his apartment.

January 2022 | Paperback | $16.99 | 9780358627982 | Mariner Books

CONVERSATION STARTERS

1. Discuss the author's note at the beginning of the novel and the tips addressed to the reader throughout. What do you make of Buck's advice? And why do you think Askaripour chose to structure the novel this way—almost like a business memoir or sales manual?

2. When Darren reverse closes Rhett at Starbucks, everything changes (13–14). What does Rhett see in Darren in that moment? Why is Darren reluctant to accept Rhett's job offer to work at Sumwun? Have you ever been afraid to pursue a new opportunity in your own life?

3. Discuss Darren's relationship to Ma, Soraya, and the "gargoyles" (Jason and Wally Cat) and how those relationships change when Darren begins working at Sumwun. How does his professional success impact his closest relationships? Have you seen anything similar happen to yourself, friends, or loved ones?

4. What is the culture like at Sumwun? What are the various rituals and hierarchies? Discuss the way Darren ("Buck") is treated compared to his colleagues as well as the ways people at the top, like Rhett and Clyde, engage with race.

5. Discuss the media's relationship to Darren—from his first TV appearance on Rise and Shine, America to Bonnie Sauren's coverage of him. What are the narratives they create for him, and how does he fight back?

6. Discuss the origins of the Happy Campers and its quick success. What does Brian offer Darren, and vice versa? What did you make of the lessons that Darren put his early members through—from the subway car entertainment to the dine and dash? What, if anything, did these scenarios teach Brian, Rose, and the rest of the crew?

7. Discuss the criticism of the Happy Campers from the White United Society of Salespeople and the media. How do they try to thwart the Happy Campers' mission? Why do they feel threatened by the Happy Campers' success?

8. Discuss your feelings toward Darren, and how they might have changed, over the course of the novel. Despite his worst actions, do you think he's ultimately redeemed?

THE BOOK OF OTTO AND LIAM
Paul Griner

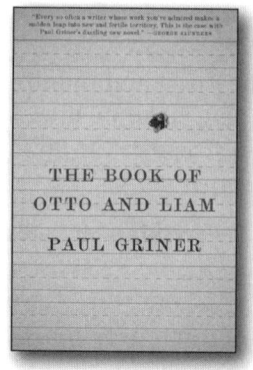

Liam is the boy, lying in the hospital, in grave condition, a bullet lodged in his head. Otto is his father, a commercial artist whose marriage has collapsed in the wake of the disaster. Paul Griner's brave novel taps directly into the vein of a uniquely American tragedy: the school shooting. We know these grotesque and sorrowful events too well. Thankfully, the characters in this drama are finely drawn human beings—those who gain our empathy, those who commit the unspeakable acts, and those conspiracy fanatics who launch a concerted campaign to convince the world that the shooting was a hoax. The Book of Otto and Liam is a suspenseful, edge-of-your-seat read and, at the same time, it is a meditation on the forms evil can take, from the irredeemable act of the shooter himself, to the anger and devastation it causes in the victims' families. Griner has managed to make an amazing, incredibly powerful book, one that is like no other..

"Dazzling" —**Man Booker Prize winner George Saunders**

"A powerful excavation into the darkest recesses of grief ... Unabashedly polemical, angry, and heartbreaking." — *Kirkus Reviews* (**starred review**)

"An entirely original portrait of grief, loss, and finding a new way forward in the aftermath of an all too-familiar tragedy." —*Booklist* (**starred review**)

"A serious and urgent book ... [it] is a portrait of us in our present moment, battered by a reckless and deceitful government, battling our own inurement to daily horrors, and doing our best to get on with the business of living." —*The Rumpus*

ABOUT THE AUTHOR: **Paul Griner** is the author of the novels *Collectors*, *The German Woman*, and *Second Life*, and the story collections *Follow Me* (a Barnes and Noble Discover Great New Writers choice) and *Hurry Please I Want to Know* (winner of the Kentucky Literary Award). He teaches writing and literature at the University of Louisville.

October 2020 | Paperback | $16.95 | 9781517910549 | Sarabande Books

CONVERSATION STARTERS

1. What makes Otto such a compelling protagonist? What are his most appealing qualities? His faults? At what crucial points in the novel does he demonstrate courage, compassion, intelligence, and/or a willingness to sacrifice himself?

2. What might Otto's obsession with Kate—from systematically searching websites for her recent videos, to trying to discover her real identity and where she lives and works—tell us about his character and state of mind? Do you think that this search is a noble struggle or a selfish one? Is justice ultimately served?

3. What do May's and Otto's individual reactions to the catastrophic events of a school shooting suggest about the nation's grief over these events? Why do you think the author chose to depict their failing marriage against the backdrop of some of the most painful moments in recent American history?

4. Otto and Liam was inspired in part by contemporary events, including numerous school shootings and the rise of "hoaxers," those who, like Alex Jones, claim that the school shootings of the last two decades never happened. How does the book capture recent transformations in American culture?

5. Most of the chapters are very short, some only a few lines. Some are in first person, some third, some are statistics, notes from hoaxers, texts, lists, poems, letters, maps, ads or illustrations, and the story is not told in a linear fashion. Why do you think the writer structured the book the way he did? Why did he include so many different types of narrative?

6. Would you say that May and Otto's qualities—intelligence, caring for others, diligence—will propel them beyond grief and a desire for revenge? Will May and Otto have a shared future?

7. One of the most complex relationships in the book is between Otto and Lamont. How would you characterize it? As Lamont seems to sink further into darkness, Otto appears to reach for a bit of light. Does he sacrifice Lamont to do so? Does he make the right choice at the end by giving Lamont Dexter Fenchwood's name?

HER HERE
Amanda Dennis

Buzz Books by Publishers Lunch selection

An atmospheric story about one lost young woman's search for another

Elena, struggling with memory loss due to a trauma that has unmoored her sense of self, deserts graduate school and a long-term relationship to accept a bizarre proposition from an estranged family friend in Paris: she will search for a young woman, Ella, who went missing six years earlier in Thailand, by rewriting her journals. As she delves deeper into Ella's story, Elena begins to lose sight of her own identity and drift dangerously toward self-annihilation.

Her Here is an existential detective story with a shocking denouement that plumbs the creative and destructive powers of narrative itself.

"*Spellbinding … Wholly engrossing … This hypnotic and deeply cerebral exploration is a seductive escape.*" —**Washington Post**

"*Dennis's elegant yet propulsive debut becomes much more than a missing-persons search … Elena's narrative-within-a-narrative nicely reveals the creative process, while Dennis's larger story confirms the value of living boldly.*" —*Library Journal* **(starred review)**

"*In* Her Here, *Dennis has written a metaphysical investigation that is also a wonderfully personal account of a daughter coming to terms with the loss of her mother, and a mother coming to terms with the loss of her daughter. As Elena conjures Ella's last days, the richly imagined narrative moves back and forth between Paris and Thailand, carrying both characters and readers to a vivid and suspenseful conclusion.*" —**Margot Livesey, author of** *The Flight of Gemma Hardy* **and** *The Boy in the Field*

ABOUT THE AUTHOR: **Amanda Dennis** is an Iowa Writers' Workshop graduate and an avid traveler who has lived in six countries, including Thailand and Paris, where she is currently assistant professor of comparative literature and creative writing at the American University of Paris. *Her Here* is her first novel.

March 2021 | Paperback | $16.99 | 9781942658764 | Bellevue Literary Press

CONVERSATION STARTERS

1. The first chapter opens with a case of mistaken identity: a stranger believes Elena is a woman she used to know. How does this scene echo the themes of memory, loss, and the longing for connection throughout the novel?

2. The title comes from a line early in the novel, when Elena first discovers Ella's journals and thinks to herself, "I'd rather be her than here." The author has described Elena's task of "translating" Ella's journals as a "quest for identity." What is Elena searching for, about both Ella and herself? How does her immersion in Ella's past influence the decisions she makes in her own life?

3. The story takes readers on a journey through the narrow streets of Paris, among the mango trees and monsoons of Thailand, and to a remote island village. How does the author use sensory details to immerse you in a place?

4. What are both Elena and Ella seeking to discover—or run away from—through travel?

5. In what ways does this story describe universal experiences that young women have coming of age? How do female friendships in the novel influence the characters' lives? Are these relationships more powerful than the romantic ones in the story?

6. The author recounts that a reader once told her "sometimes the mother-daughter bond can hold more tension than a love affair," and much of the book centers on the theme of motherhood. Who are the mother or surrogate mother figures in the characters' lives, and what roles do they play? How do you think Elena's relationship with Ella's mother might evolve after the story ends?

7. What happens to Ella in Elena's telling of her story? What really happens to her? Do you think the two versions are the same?

8. The publisher describes *Her Here* as "an existential detective story," author Alexandra Kleeman calls it "a ghost story without a ghost," and a bookseller compared it to the suspenseful fiction of Gillian Flynn. How would you describe the plot twists and psychological revelations within the novel? Did you anticipate the ending?

THE HOUSE OF RUST
Khadija Abdalla Bajaber

The first Graywolf Press African Fiction Prize winner, a story of a girl's fantastical sea voyage to rescue her father

The House of Rust is an enchanting novel about a Hadrami girl in Mombasa. When her fisherman father goes missing, Aisha takes to the sea on a magical boat made of a skeleton to rescue him. She is guided by a talking scholar's cat (and soon crows, goats, and other animals all have their say, too). On this journey Aisha meets three terrifying sea monsters. After she survives a final confrontation with Baba wa Papa, the father of all sharks, she rescues her own father, and hopes that life will return to normal. But at home, things only grow stranger. Khadija Abdalla Bajaber's debut is a fabulist coming-of-age tale told through the lens of the Swahili and diasporic Hadrami culture in Mombasa, Kenya. Richly descriptive and written with an imaginative hand and sharp eye for unusual detail, *The House of Rust* is a memorable novel by a thrilling new voice.

"A novel stuffed to bursting with marvels and fairy-tale delights. Khadija Abdalla Bajaber casts a mighty spell." —**Kelly Link**

"Khadija Abdalla Bajaber's command of language and story is transcendent. *The House of Rust* is an immersive experience in Kenyan mythology, and an honest exploration of loss and family from a uniquely talented writer." —**Wayétu Moore**

"*The House of Rust* is a gorgeous coming-of-age story, and I'm going to be obsessing about it for quite some time ... I wanted to lose myself forever in the dark spaces of Khadija Abdalla Bajaber's prose." —**Charlie Jane Anders**

ABOUT THE AUTHOR: **Khadija Abdalla Bajaber** is a Mombasarian writer of Hadrami descent and the winner of the inaugural Graywolf Press African Fiction Prize. Her work has appeared in *Enkare Review, Lohwe*, and *Down River Road* among other places. She lives in Mombasa, Kenya.

October 2021 | Paperback | $16.00 | 9781644450680 | Graywolf Press

CONVERSATION STARTERS

1. The coastal city of Mombasa, Kenya is an important character in *The House of Rust*. What did you know about Mombasa before starting the novel? If you are less familiar with it, take some time to read about the city from a few outside sources. How do these facts relate to what you read in the novel?

2. How is *The House of Rust* like other quest narratives you have encountered? How is it different?

3. Who are the heroes and who are the villains in this story? Are these clear and simple distinctions?

4. What roles do animals and monsters play in the novel? How does this change throughout the course of the book?

5. *The House of Rust* pays close attention to lineages and inheritance. What are examples of things passed on between generations? Does this transfer ever occur from younger to older generations?

6. How does food show up as an important detail in the text? What aspects of this cuisine were familiar to you, and what aspects were new? Did the novel make you want to try Swahili food?

7. Khadija Abdalla Bajaber skillfully depicts how characters' inner lives and thoughts conflict or diverge from their speech and actions, which are so often influenced by the roles they are expected to play. Give some examples of the secret lives these characters carry within. How do some of these tensions resolve and come into the light as events unfold?

8. On page 128, Zubeir tells Aisha, "You say you don't understand when you mean to say you don't know how you feel or can't accept it." Name several instances in which characters take journeys or expend great effort just to understand knowledge they already carried within themselves.

9. Is the House of Rust a real place? What do you imagine it to be like?

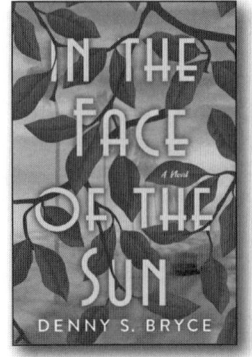

IN THE FACE OF THE SUN
Denny S. Bryce

At the height of the Civil Rights Movement amidst an America convulsed by the 1960s, a pregnant young woman and her brash, profane aunt embark upon an audacious road trip from Chicago to Los Angeles to confront a decades-old mystery from 1920's Black Hollywood in this haunting novel of historical fiction from the author of Wild Women and the Blues.

1928, Los Angeles: The newly-built Hotel Somerville is the hotspot for the city's glittering African-American elite. It embodies prosperity and dreams of equality for all—especially Daisy Washington. An up-and-coming journalist, Daisy anonymously chronicles fierce activism and behind-the-scenes Hollywood scandals in order to save her family from poverty. But power in the City of Angels is also fueled by racism, greed, and betrayal. And even the most determined young woman can play too many secrets too far ...

1968, Chicago: For Frankie Saunders, fleeing across America is her only escape from an abusive husband. But her rescuer is her reckless, profane Aunt Daisy, still reeling from her own shattered past. Frankie doesn't want to know what her aunt is up to so long as Daisy can get her to LA—and safety. But Frankie finds there's no hiding from long-held secrets—or her own surprising strength.

Daisy will do whatever it takes to settle old scores and resolve the past—no matter the damage. And Frankie will come up against hard choices in the face of unexpected passion. Both must come to grips with what they need, what they've left behind—and all that lies ahead ...

ABOUT THE AUTHOR: **Denny S. Bryce** is an award-winning author and three-time RWA Golden Heart® finalist. A member of Tall Poppy Writers, the Historical Novel Society, Women's Fiction Writers Association, and Novelists, Inc., she also writes for NPR Books and FROLIC Media. She lives in Georgia and can be found online at www.DennySBryce.com.

April 2020 | Paperback | $15.95 | 9781496730107 | Kensington Books

CONVERSATION STARTERS

1. Many have heard of some of the pioneers of Black Hollywood, actors such as Hattie McDaniel, Paul Robson, Butterfly McQueen and Dorothy Dandridge. What major obstacles do you think Black actors faced in the 1920s and 1930s? How do these challenges compare to what is happening in Hollywood today?

2. During the 1920's and beyond, Black newspapers and magazines were a critical source of information, especially with regards to the events, actions, and people effecting the rights of the Black community. Are you familiar with any past or presently published Black newspapers? How do you think the significance and role of the Black press has changed since the 1920s?

3. Due to the draft, the Vietnam War had a personal impact on nearly every family and community throughout the 1960s. As young men were forced into military service by the hundreds of thousands, this impact was felt in varying ways throughout the country. Do you think the Vietnam War effected Black Americans differently from the rest of the country? If so, how?

4. The four main characters in this novel are women experiencing various stages of grief, discovery, love, and forgiveness. In what ways does the Hotel Somerville serve as a metaphor for these themes?

5. The Hotel Somerville eventually became the Dunbar Hotel, the cornerstone of the Los Angeles Jazz scene from the 1920s through the 1940s. What is the role of music in the novel's 1928 storyline versus the 1968 storyline?

6. Several characters in this novel face various forms of abuse: physical, emotional, and racial, for example. How would you describe the long-term effects of abuse on an individual, male or female, versus its impact on a culture, gender, or ethnic group?

7. Sometimes referred to as "The Year that Changed America Forever," 1968 was a year filled with significant events, turmoil, and tragedies. What events in 1968 do you think had the largest impact on the nation and the African American community in particular?

THE JANE AUSTEN SOCIETY
Natalie Jenner

Just after the Second World War, in the small English village of Chawton, an unusual but likeminded group of people band together to attempt something remarkable.

One hundred and fifty years ago, Chawton was the final home of Jane Austen, one of England's finest novelists. Now it's home to a few distant relatives and their diminishing estate. With the last bit of Austen's legacy threatened, a group of disparate individuals come together to preserve both Jane Austen's home and her legacy. These people—a laborer, a young widow, the local doctor, and a movie star, among others—could not be more different and yet they are united in their love for the works and words of Austen. As each of them endures their own quiet struggle with loss and trauma, some from the recent war, others from more distant tragedies, they rally together to create the Jane Austen Society.

A powerful and moving novel that explores the tragedies and triumphs of life, both large and small, and the universal humanity in us all, Natalie Jenner's *The Jane Austen Society* is destined to resonate with readers for years to come.

"This novel delivers sweet, smart escapism." —*People*

"Fans of *The Chilbury Ladies' Choir* and *The Guernsey Literary and Potato Peel Pie Society* will adore *The Jane Austen Society*." —**Pam Jenoff**, *New York Times* **bestselling author of** *The Lost Girls of Paris*

ABOUT THE AUTHOR: **Natalie Jenner** born in England, raised in Canada, and graduated from the University of Toronto with consecutive degrees in English Literature and Law. She worked for decades in the legal industry and also founded the independent bookstore Archetype Books in Oakville, Ontario, where she lives with her family and two rescue dogs. A lifelong devotee of all things Jane Austen, *The Jane Austen Society* is her first published novel.

May 2020 | Harcover | $26.99 | 9781250248732 | St. Martin's Press
July 2021 | Paperback | $16.99 | 9781250797179 | St. Martin's Griffin

CONVERSATION STARTERS

1. There is a wide range of major characters in *The Jane Austen Society*. Which of the eight main characters was your favorite? Which of their personal stories did you find the most satisfying? Which one do you most identify with and why?

2. Jane Austen's writing – and the characters' love of her writing – is what brings them together. If you are a fan of Jane Austen, what is your favorite book and why? If not, then which of her books are you now most interested in reading?

3. Several of the characters are living with – and, to differing extents, dealing with – the grief of losing a close loved one. Did you find yourself sympathizing with one of them more than the others? What about their story touched you the most?

4. Most of *The Jane Austen Society* takes place in the 1940s, right after World War II. Given that it was a very different time, with very different attitudes, what aspect revealed in the novel seemed the most familiar to your experience? What seemed the most changed since that time?

5. Mimi Harrison is in sharp contrast to the rest of the characters – she's from the U.S., she's a movie star, she has wealth far beyond the rest of the characters. Beyond their shared love of Jane Austen's work, what traits do you think she has most in common with the rest of the characters? Which other character does she best complement?

6. Adam Berwick has to make an important decision – one that will not only affect the Society but his family as well. Do you think he made the right decision? Why?

7. There are many obvious and more subtle allusions to Austen's own plots and characters throughout the book. If you're familiar with Austen, which parallels did you particularly notice? Which ones most delighted you?

8. What do you imagine happened to the society and to the members after the end of the book?

LEAVE THE WORLD BEHIND
Rumaan Alam

A Read with Jenna Today Show Book Club Pick

Finalist for the 2020 National Book Award

A magnetic novel about two families, strangers to each other, who are forced together on a long weekend gone terribly wrong.

From the bestselling author of *Rich and Pretty* comes a suspenseful and provocative novel keenly attuned to the complexities of parenthood, race, and class. Leave the World Behind explores how our closest bonds are reshaped—and unexpected new ones are forged—in moments of crisis.

Amanda and Clay head out to a remote corner of Long Island expecting a vacation: a quiet reprieve from life in New York City, quality time with their teenage son and daughter, and a taste of the good life in the luxurious home they've rented for the week. But a late-night knock on the door breaks the spell. Ruth and G. H. are an older couple—it's their house, and they've arrived in a panic. They bring the news that a sudden blackout has swept the city. But in this rural area—with the TV and internet now down, and no cell phone service—it's hard to know what to believe.

Should Amanda and Clay trust this couple—and vice versa? What happened back in New York? Is the vacation home, isolated from civilization, a truly safe place for their families? And are they safe from one other?

ABOUT THE AUTHOR: **Rumaan Alam** is the author of the novels *Rich and Pretty*, *That Kind of Mother*, and the instant *New York Times* bestseller *Leave the World Behind*. His writing has appeared in *The New York Times*, *New York Magazine*, *The New Yorker*, *The New York Review of Books*, *Bookforum*, and the *New Republic*, where he is a contributing editor. He studied writing at Oberlin College and lives in New York with his family.

October 2020 | Hardcover | $27.99 | 9780062667632 | Ecco
November 2021 | Paperback | $16.99 | 9780062667649 | Ecco

CONVERSATION STARTERS

1. What were your first impressions of Amanda and Clay? Ruth and G. H.? Did your understanding of them change as the novel progressed, or did they uphold your initial expectations?

2. *Leave the World Behind* is a work of fiction, written before the COVID-19 outbreak and the societal uprisings that shaped 2020. If you had read the novel before 2020, do you think you would have had a different response to it? If so, in what way?

3. For much of the novel, Amanda, Clay, Ruth, and G. H. can't agree on whether or not they are truly in danger. Why do you think they found it so hard to assess their situation? What would you have done if you were in the shoes of Amanda and Clay? Ruth and G. H.?

4. Ruth and G. H. are separated from their daughter and grandsons for the duration of the crisis, while Amanda and Clay have their kids with them. Do you think that changes their response to the situation they are facing together?

5. How do you think the children, Archie and Rose, see the world in comparison to their parents? Do they share a similar vision of it? If not, how so?

6. In *Leave the World Behind*, the families grapple with the sudden loss of communications technology—cell phone, internet, and satellite services all fail. What is your relationship to technology? Do you embrace it? Do you wish our society handled its role in our lives differently?

7. This novel pairs two couples together who are from different demographic backgrounds in terms of race and wealth. How did those qualities impact the way they interact with one another?

8. What do you think this book says about the role of friends and neighbors? Do you think these characters will have to fend for themselves, or is there hope that they will have others to lean on? What do you think happens to these families after the book ends?

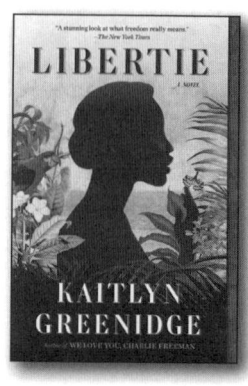

LIBERTIE
Kaitlyn Greenidge

Coming of age in a free Black community in Reconstruction-era Brooklyn, Libertie Sampson is all too aware that her mother, a practicing physician, has a vision for their future together: Libertie is to go to medical school and practice alongside her. But Libertie, drawn more to music than science, feels stifled by her mother's choices and is hungry for something else. And she is constantly reminded that, unlike her light-skinned mother, Libertie will not be able to pass for white. When a young man from Haiti proposes to Libertie and promises she will be his equal on the island, she accepts, only to discover that she is still subordinate to him and all men. As she tries to parse what freedom actually means for a Black woman, Libertie struggles with where she might find it—for herself and for generations to come.

Inspired by the life of one of the first Black female doctors in the United States, Kaitlyn Greenidge's new novel will resonate with readers eager to understand our present through a deep dive into our past.

"This immersive story is a soaring exploration of what 'freedom' truly means. Libertie *is an elegantly layered, beautifully rendered tour de force that is not to be missed."* —**Roxane Gay**

"Spectacular ... A revelatory and enchanting piece of historical fiction." —*Buzzfeed*

"A feat of monumental thematic imagination." —**Margaret Wilkerson Sexton,** *The New York Times Book Review*

"Amazingly beautiful .... Greenidge is a master storyteller." —**Jacqueline Woodson, author of** *Red at the Bone*

ABOUT THE AUTHOR: **Kaitlyn Greenidge**'s debut novel, *We Love You, Charlie Freeman*, was one of the *New York Times* Critics' Top 10 Books of 2016. She is the features director at *Harper's Bazaar*, and her writing has appeared in the *New York Times*, *Vogue*, and elsewhere. She is the recipient of fellowships from the Guggenheim Foundation, the Whiting Foundation, and the National Endowment for the Arts. Greenidge lives in Massachusetts.

March 2021 | Hardcover | $26.95 | 9781616207014 | Algonquin Books
March 2022 | Paperback | $16.95 | 9781643752587 | Algonquin Books

CONVERSATION STARTERS

1. *Libertie* grew out of Kaitlyn Greenidge's research about Dr. Susan Smith McKinney Steward and her daughter. Although the characters take their origins from Steward and her daughter Anna, Greenidge expands deeply on the historical record. Why do you think she chose to write this as fiction rather than nonfiction?

2. Ben Daisy tells Libertie that his girlfriend "said if she were ever free, she'd spend all day covered in silk and she'd paint her face pretty ... She knew what she would do with freedom. It wasn't man's work she'd do with freedom. Not like your mama. She knew better than that." And Emmanuel Chase also has a specific definition of freedom in relation to women. How is freedom defined in the novel by men? How is it defined by women?

3. Libertie is much darker skinned than her mother, as many people remark to each of them. How does that physical fact influence Libertie's perspective on the world? How does it inform her choices?

4. After such a clear passion for medicine and for following her mother's path, Libertie changes her mind and decides she does not want to become a doctor. Why?

5. When Cathy Sampson opens the hospital, she makes a number of compromises. How do you feel about her choices?

6. In what ways do the Graces influence Libertie?

7. Why doesn't Cathy want Libertie to marry Emmanuel Chase? She says to Libertie, "You chose your body over your mind." Do you agree with her assessment of Libertie's decision? What does she fear for her daughter?

8. How did you end up feeling about Emmanuel?

9. In many ways, this novel is about the relationship between mothers and their children. Discuss Cathy and Libertie's dynamic, and what Libertie hopes for her own children. Did you feel more drawn to Cathy or to Libertie?

10. Libertie is named by her father "in honor of the bright, shining future he was sure was coming." How do you feel about Libertie's future by the close of the novel?

LITTLE FOXES TOOK UP MATCHES
Katya Kazbek

A powerful story of sexual awakening and acceptance voiced by an unforgettable protagonist coming of age in post-Soviet Russia.

When Mitya was two years old, he swallowed his grandmother's sewing needle. For his family, it marks the beginning of the end, the promise of certain death. For Mitya, it is a small, metal treasure that guides him from within. As he grows, his life mirrors the uncertain future of his country, which is attempting to rebuild itself after the collapse of the Soviet Union, torn between its past and the promise of modern freedom. Mitya finds himself facing a different sort of ambiguity: is he a boy, as everyone keeps telling him, or is he not quite a boy, as he often feels?

After suffering horrific abuse from his cousin Vovka who has returned broken from war, Mitya embarks on a journey across underground Moscow to find something better, a place to belong. His experiences are interlaced with a retelling of a foundational Russian fairytale, Koschei the Deathless, offering an element of fantasy to the brutal realities of Mitya's everyday life.

Told with deep empathy, humor, and a bit of surreality, *Little Foxes Took Up Matches* is a revelation about the life of one community in a country of turmoil and upheaval, glimpsed through the eyes of a precocious and empathetic child, whose heart and mind understand that there are often more than two choices. An arresting coming of age, an exploration of gender, a modern folktale, a comedy about family—Katya Kazbeck breaks out as a new voice to watch.

ABOUT THE AUTHOR: **Katya Kazbek** is a bilingual Russian/English writer, translator and editor based in NYC. Kazbek has worked as a fashion writer, with articles appearing in *Russian GQ*, *Vogue.ru*. She co-founded the online magazine *Supamodu.com* and her writing has appeared in *Creative Time Reports* and *Guernica*. A previous graduate of Parsons and Oxford's writing program, Kazbek received her MFA from Columbia University.

April 2022 | Hardcover | $ 26.95 | 9781953534026 | TinHouse

CONVERSATION STARTERS

1. *Little Foxes Took Up Matches* opens with an introduction of Koschei the Deathless, and the folktale is woven throughout the novel—what does the fable add to Mitya's story, both narratively and atmospherically?

2. The needle is a symbol throughout the narrative. What did it symbolize to Mitya? To Mitya's family? To you?

3. Animals—crows, bees, foxes—also play an important role in the novel. What roles do they play in the story?

4. How does the neighborhood of Arbat, and Moscow as a whole, become an important character in the novel? What parts of the city are revealed to the reader?

5. How are historical events surrounding the collapse of the Soviet Union described through Mitya's youthful perspective?

6. While left alone at home, Mitya decides to "explore the secret lives of his parents and grandmother." How do personal and family secrets play a role in Mitya's coming-of-age?

7. How would you characterize Mitya's friendship with Marina? Who did you confide in most when you were young?

8. In an important moment of introspection, Mitya thinks that "he was the only one who could make everything right if he only believed in himself enough." Has there been a moment in your life where you were your best advocate?

9. In what ways would this novel be different if it were written in first-person point-of-view?

10. What are your hopes for Mitya after the novel ends?

THE MOVEMENT
Petra Hůlová, translated by Alex Zucker

The Movement's founding ideology emphasizes that women should be valued for their inner qualities, spirit, and character, and not for their physical attributes. Men have been forbidden to be attracted to women on the basis of their bodies. Some continue with unreformed attitudes but many submit—or are sent by their wives and daughters—to the Institute for internment and reeducation. However, the Movement also struggles with women and their "old attitudes," with many still undergoing illegal cosmetic surgeries and wearing makeup. Our narrator, an unapologetic guard at one of these reeducation facilities, describes how the Movement started, the challenges faced, her own personal journey, and what happens when a program fails. She is convinced the Movement is nearing its final victory—a time when everybody falls in line with its ideals. Outspoken, ambiguous, and terrifying, this socio-critical satire of our sexual norms sets the reader firmly outside of their comfort zone.

"Petra Hůlová is one of the most distinctive and outspoken Czech writers of her generation." —*Project Plume*

"In a dystopian future where women rule, society is re-educated to teach men—and women—that women should be valued for traits other than their appearance or age. The novel is dark and satirical; while feminism is in the foreground, the author somehow manages a balancing act between manifesto and critique." —*Lithub*

"A thought-provoking and disturbing dystopian tale of a feminist revolution." —*Publishers Weekly*

ABOUT THE AUTHOR: **Petra Hůlová**'s provocative novels, plays, and screenplays have won numerous awards, including the ALTA National Translation Award for Alex Zucker's translation of her debut novel, *All This Belongs to Me*, and she is a regular commentator on current events for the Czech press. Her eight novels and three plays have been translated into thirteen languages. *A Brief History of the Movement* is her latest novel.

Octobert 2021 | Paperback | $16.00 | 9781642861006 | World Editions

CONVERSATION STARTERS

1. Would you describe the world of this book as a dystopia, a utopia, or somewhere in between, and why?
2. Do you agree/disagree with the ideals of the Movement?
3. Do you think the society described in this novel is better or worse than the society you live in? And in what ways?
4. Do you think the events of this novel describe a realistic future possibility?
5. Do you think the narrator, Vera, is a reliable narrator? What are her biases? Do you think she is in touch with her own emotions?
6. Did you spot any rhetorical sleights of hand in Vera's ideologically colored comments?
7. In your view, were they innocuous tools to highlight the positive and righteous elements in her point of view? Or did you perhaps even see signs of cognitive dissonance?
8. Vera's past is only subtly hinted at within the book, but what can you glean from these hints? Is there anything in her past that could explain her current character?
9. Do you think she is lonely, happy; how might you describe her?
10. Do you think the system of treatment organized by the Movement works? Or do you think the men are likely to relapse once they return to their normal lives?
11. Do you think the system of treatment is humane, or does it violate certain rights? Or, in your opinion, do the women of the Movement perhaps have a right to treat men in such a way?
12. Do you think the treatment is more likely to be effective on men or women? And, if you see a difference between the two, why do you think that is?
13. If you were a member of such a Movement, how would you do things differently?
14. What do you think about the men's opposition groups? Do you agree/disagree with their ideals? Or do you think perhaps that both sides in some ways are in the right?

THE MYSTERIES
Marisa Silver

From the *New York Times* bestselling author of *Mary Coin*, a masterful, intimate story of two young girls, joined in an unlikely friendship, whose lives are shattered in a single, unthinkable moment.

Miggy Brenneman is a wild and reckless seven-year-old with a fierce imagination, hellbent on pushing against the limits of childhood. Ellen is polite, cautious, and drawn to her friend's bright flame. While the adults around them adjust to unstable times and fractured relationships, the girls respond with increasingly dangerous play. When tragedy strikes, all the novel's characters grapple with questions of fate and individual responsibility, none more so than Miggy, who must make sense of a swiftly disappearing past and a radically transformed future.

Written with searing clarity and surpassing tenderness, *The Mysteries* limns the painful ambiguities of adulthood and the intense perceptions of an indelibly drawn child to offer a profound exploration of how all of us, at every stage, must reckon with life's abundant and unsolvable mysteries.

"Family and friendship are the central mysteries of Silver's latest novel, which is set against the tumult of the early 1970s and features a fraught bond between young girls." —*The New York Times Book Review*

"Marisa Silver uses language as she would a sharp needle: to stitch, and to puncture, in her examination of people." —**Rachel Kushner**, *New York Times* bestselling author of *The Mars Room*

"This exquisite gem of a novel digs deep into the longings of the human heart."
—**Cynthia D'Aprix Sweeney**, *New York Times* bestselling author of *The Nest*

ABOUT THE AUTHOR: **Marisa Silver** is the author of six previous works of fiction, including the novels *Mary Coin*, a *New York Times* Bestseller, and *Little Nothing*, a *New York Times* Editor's Choice. Her short fiction has appeared in *The New Yorker* and been included in *The Best American Short Stories* and The O. Henry Prize Stories. Silver has received fellowships from the Guggenheim Foundation and the New York Public Library's Cullman Center. She teaches at the MFA Program for Writers at Warren Wilson College and lives in Los Angeles.

May 2021 | Hardcover | $26.00 | 9781635576443 | Bloomsbury

CONVERSATION STARTERS

1. The novel is told in multiple points of view and follows members of both families. What effect does this have on the reader? What does the reader gain by being inside all of the characters' perspectives?

2. Consider the novel's epigraph: "Never childhood to a child." How does this statement apply to Miggy's experiences and selfconception?

3. How does Silver change her style and voice when depicting a child's interiority? Did you find her portrayals of children to be realistic and successful? Why do you think Silver chose to enter the childrens' points of view as well as the adults'?

4. Describe the changes that occur in Miggy's character. How does her short relationship with Ellen, and Ellen's ensuing absence, affect her formation of an identity? To what extent are her maturation and loss of innocence universal experiences, and in what ways are they brought about by her specific circumstances?

5. Though Ellen and Miggy are only seven their relationship contains many complexities and fraught moments, like when Miggy ties Ellen with a jump rope, or when Miggy barges/goes into Celeste's room despite Ellen's dismay. How do their games and their relationship reflect the conflicts within their families?

6. Silver explores the history, geography, and gentrification of St. Louis, particularly in relation to Julian's hardware store and its neighbors. Discuss the prominence of the setting within the narrative. How does the city impact the character's conceptions of their own identities?

7. Jean feels conflicted about both the nascent feminism of the 1970s and her gendered domestic duties, while Celeste mostly ignores those duties in the haze of postpartum depression. Julian and William both carry the financial burden for their families in careers that respond to their respective fathers' legacies. How do traditional notions of gender play out in the lives of each of these couples? How is Celeste, in her depression and her grief, affected by expectations of femininity? How is Jean?

8. What are the mysteries in the novel? How do they differ for each character?

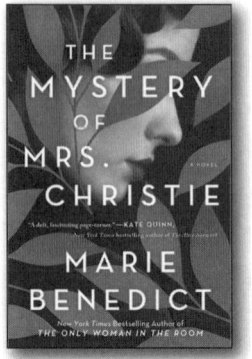

THE MYSTERY OF MRS. CHRISTIE
Marie Benedict

The Instant *New York Times* **and** *USA Today* **Bestseller**

December 1926: England unleashes the largest manhunt in its history. The object of the search is not an escaped convict or a war criminal, but the missing wife of a WWI hero, up-and-coming mystery author Agatha Christie.

When her car is found wrecked, empty, and abandoned near a natural spring, the country is in a frenzy. Eleven days later, Agatha reappears, claiming amnesia. She provides no answers for her disappearance. That is ... until she writes a very strange book about a missing woman, a murderous husband, and a plan to expose the truth. What role did her unfaithful husband play? And what was he not telling investigators?

The Mystery of Mrs. Christie explores one strong woman's successful endeavor to write her own narrative and take her history into her own hands.

"Stunning ... The ending is ingenious, and it's possible that Benedict has brought to life the most plausible explanation for why Christie disappeared for 11 days in 1926." —*Washington Post*

"A whodunit infinitely worthy of its famous heroine. Benedict's exploration of Agatha Christie's life and mysterious disappearance will have book club discussions running overtime." —Lisa Wingate, #1 *New York Times* **bestselling author of** *Before We Were Yours* **and** *The Book of Lost Friends*

"A deft, fascinating page-turner replete with richly drawn characters and plot twists that would stump Hercule Poirot." —Kate Quinn, *New York Times* **bestselling author of** *The Alice Network*, *The Huntress*, **and** *The Rose Code*

ABOUT THE AUTHOR: **Marie Benedict** is a lawyer with more than ten years' experience as a litigator, and is the author of *The Other Einstein*, *Carnegie's Maid*, *The Only Woman in the Room*, and *Lady Clementine*. Marie views herself as an archaeologist of sorts, telling the untold stories of women. She lives in Pittsburgh with her family.

December 2020 | Hardcover | $26.99 | 9781492682721 | Sourcebooks Landmark
October 2021 | Paperback | $16.99 | 9781728234304 | Sourcebooks Landmark

CONVERSATION STARTERS

1. Agatha Christie is one of the most celebrated mystery writers of all time. What did you know about her personal history before you read The Mystery of Mrs. Christie? Did the book challenge any of your preconceived notions about her life?

2. Agatha Christie was a successful writer within her lifetime, quite unusual for a woman of her time. How did her desire for independence shape the course of the story, both obviously and more subtly?

3. Do you think Agatha Christie is a good representative of the issues that women faced in her era? Did she have any privileges or responsibilities that set her apart from other women of her period?

4. Describe the night Archie and Agatha first met. How did their relationship change over time, and why? Do you think Agatha's manuscript told the full story? What details do you think she changed or left out? Why do you think she might have altered the "truth"?

5. Archie spends much of the story trying to protect his reputation. Do you think that would be the case if the story took place today? Would it be easier or more difficult for him to deflect guilt in the modern news cycle?

6. What differences did you see between the Agatha within the manuscript and the Agatha who appears at the end of the book? What creative licenses did she take with her own personality and story? Were they justified?

7. Which characters, if any, did you find to be most relatable? Did you connect with Agatha? Were there any characters you wished you knew more about?

8. Agatha left an enormous mark on the mystery community and on the world of books more generally. Do you think her marriage had an effect on her success? Or her disappearance? If so, what was it? How would you characterize her personal and professional legacies?

NIGHTBITCH
Rachel Yoder

In this blazingly smart and voracious debut, an artist turned stay-at-home mom becomes convinced she's turning into a dog.

An ambitious mother puts her art career on hold to stay home with her newborn son. Two years later, she steps into the bathroom for a break from her toddler's demands, only to discover a dense patch of hair on the back of her neck and unusually sharp canines. Her husband, who travels for work, casually dismisses her fears from faraway hotel rooms.

As the mother's symptoms intensify, she struggles to keep her alter-canine-identity secret. Seeking a cure at the library, she discovers the mysterious academic tome, *A Field Guide to Magical Women: A Mythical Ethnography*, and meets a group of mothers involved in a multilevel-marketing scheme who may also be more than what they seem.

An outrageously original novel of ideas about art, power, and womanhood wrapped in a satirical fairy tale, *Nightbitch* will make you want to howl in laughter and recognition. And you should. You should howl as much as you want.

"A uniquely brilliant book ... magical, dark, and funny." —**Kevin Wilson**

"Feral, unholy ... Nightbitch *is an incredible feat.*" —**Carmen Maria Machado**

"A high wire act of a novel that expertly balances the uncanny and quotidian moments of early motherhood. Graceful, funny and unnerving as hell." —**Jenny Offill**

"Bursting with fury, loneliness, and vulgarity, Yoder's narrative revels in its deconstruction of the social script women and mothers are taught to follow ... An electric work by an ingenious new voice." —***Publishers Weekly*** **(starred review)**

A battle hymn as novel about sinking your teeth into the available options for self-determination and ripping them to shreds." —***Kirkus Reviews***

ABOUT THE AUTHOR: **Rachel Yoder** is a founding editor of draft: the journal of process. She holds MFAs from the University of Arizona (fiction) and the University of Iowa (nonfiction). She lives in Iowa City with her husband and son.

July 2021 | Hardcover | $26.00 | 9780385546812 | Doubleday

CONVERSATION STARTERS

1. Does the main character actually transform into a dog, or is the transformation a fantasy of Nightbitch's sleep-deprived mind? Does it matter whether the transformation is "real" or not?

2. In the book, the main character is only referred to as "the mother" or "Nightbitch." Similarly, the husband and the son are both also left unnamed. Why do you suppose this is? What effect did it have on your reading of the book?

3. After an animalistic act of violence, the book lapses into extended backstory about Nightbitch's childhood and mother. How does the information in this section add to your understanding of Nightbitch and her own story of motherhood?

4. The "performance of motherhood" is an idea that's played with in this book. Where do you see this idea being animated in the book and what does this animation have to say about the nature of modern motherhood?

5. What are all the different ways in which you see creativity being manifested in this book? What are the parallels between raising a child and making a piece of art?

6. What are the messages Nightbitch has received about what a "good mother" is and how does she ultimately redefine this for herself? In the end, how do you think Nightbitch would define "good mother" for herself?

7. Can you explain how humor worked within a scene in *Nightbitch*? What are the benefits of including humor in such a dark and in many regards serious book?

8. From the idea of "working moms" to the herbal multi-level marketing scheme, how does capitalism affect contemporary notions of motherhood and how Nightbitch feels about herself as a woman and a mother?

9. How did the husband's behavior contribute to Nightbitch's evolution? And how and why do you think his behavior changed as the Mother became more Nightbitch?

10. What would have been lost if Wanda White and her book weren't a part of Nightbitch's story? What function does this phantom character play within the book?

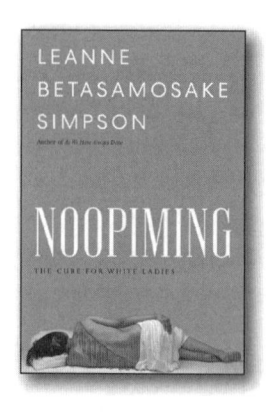

NOOPIMING: THE CURE FOR WHITE LADIES
Leanne Betasamosake Simpson

In fierce prose and poetic fragments, Leanne Betasamosake Simpson's *Noopiming* braids together humor, piercing detail, and a deep, abiding commitment to Anishinaabe life to tell stories of resistance, love, and joy. Mashkawaji (they/them) lies frozen in the ice, remembering the sharpness of unmuted feeling from long ago, finding freedom and solace in isolated suspension. They introduce the seven characters: Akiwenzii, the old man who represents the narrator's will; Ninaatig, the maple tree who represents their lungs; Mindimooyenh, the old woman, their conscience; Sabe, a gentle giant, their marrow; Adik, the caribou, their nervous system; and Asin and Lucy, the humans who represent their eyes, ears, and brain. A bold literary act of decolonization and resistance, *Noopiming* offers a breaking open of the self to a world alive with people, animals, ancestors, and spirits—and the daily work of healing.

"Leanne Betasamosake Simpson's Noopiming *once again confirms her position as a brilliant, daring experimentalist and a beautiful, radical portraitist of contemporary NDN life. The prose hums with a lovingness that moved me to tears and with a humor that felt plucked right out of my rez adolescence."* —**Billy-Ray Belcourt, award-winning author of** *This Wound Is a World* **and** *NDN Coping Mechanisms*

"I'm pretty sure we don't deserve Leanne Betasamosake Simpson. But miracles happen, and this is one. This book is poem, novel, prophecy, handbook, and side-eyed critique all at once." —**Alexis Pauline Gumbs, author of** *Dub: Finding Ceremony*

"The tenderness and sly wit of these snippets coalesce into a beautiful image of Native resilience and a piercing, original novel." —**Publishers Weekly**

"Probably unlike anything you've ever read ... remarkable." —**Ms. Magazine**

ABOUT THE AUTHOR: **Leanne Betasamosake Simpson** is a Michi Saagiig Nishnaabeg writer, scholar, and musician. A member of Alderville First Nation in Ontario, she is author of several books, including *As We Have Always Done* and *This Accident of Being Lost*.

February 2021 | Hardcover | $24.95 | 9781517911256 | University of Minnesota Press

CONVERSATION STARTERS

1. The seven main characters in *Noopiming*, in addition to Maskawaji, use they/them pronouns. How does this impact the reader's experience of gender in the book?

2. *Noopiming* takes place in the present. The characters in the novel often shatter contemporary stereotypes and portrayal of Native American and Indigenous peoples. How does this book break open the idea of a novel and how Indigenous stories can be told?

3. Simpson uses satire and humor throughout the book to critique contemporary life. What are some examples of this from the text and how does this enhance the reader's experience?

4. *Noopiming* challenges the reader's idea of linear time and the demarcations of past/present/future in many ways. What is Simpson doing with western ideas of time?

5. Simpson challenges the borders between rural and urban space by setting the story in cities, on reserves, in parks, and in the bush. How does this emphasize the idea that all land is Indigenous land?

6. The cover image is by Anishinaabe artist Rebecca Belmore and is entitled "Fringe." How do you think this image relates to the themes of the novel?

7. The music video "Solidification" (z.umn.edu/solidification) is a musical and visual interpretation of the beginning of the novel, from Simpson's album Noopiming Sessions (z.umn.edu/noopimingsessions). How do these artistic projects help Noopiming to travel? Does "Solidification" deepen your understanding of the novel?

8. Simpson uses her language Nishnaabemowin throughout the book, and doesn't translate the words into English, instead directing readers to an online Ojibwe dictionary. Why do you think she made this decision?

9. Canadian writers Margaret Atwood and Carol Shields have both written works related to Susanna Moodie and *Roughing It in the Bush*. How does Simpson's novel relate to this historic work and what do you think she is trying to say about this relationship?

10. Tragedy and trauma exist on the margins of this story. What meaning do you think Simpson is trying to convey to readers by writing adjacent to trauma rather than centering it?

OLGA DIES DREAMING
Xochitl Gonzalez

A blazing talent debuts with the tale of a status-driven wedding planner grappling with her social ambitions, absent mother, and Puerto Rican roots, all in the wake of Hurricane Maria.

"The extraordinary accomplishment of Olga Dies Dreaming *is in how a familiar-enough tale—a woman seeking love, happiness, and fulfillment in the big city—slowly reveals itself to be something else altogether."* —**Rumaan Alam, author of** *Leave the World Behind*

"In this sparkling debut, Gonzalez digs deep into the damaged heart of a family, ably dissecting the knottiness of conditional love, identity, loyalty, secrets and the very definition of home." —**Cynthia Sweeney, author of** *The Nest and Good Company*

"Olga Dies Dreaming is the story of an imperfect family shattered by secrets, grief, and abandonment, and of people who rise up, refusing to be broken." —**Jaquira Díaz, author of** *Ordinary Girls*

ABOUT THE AUTHOR: **Xochitl Gonzalez** received her MFA from the Iowa Writers' Workshop, where she was an Iowa Arts Fellow and the recipient of the Michener-Copernicus Fellowship for Fiction. Prior to writing, Xochitl wore many hats, including entrepreneur, wedding planner, fundraiser and tarot card reader. She is a proud alumna of the New York City public school system and holds a BA in art history and visual art from Brown University. She lives in her hometown of Brooklyn with her dog, Hectah Lavoe.

January 2020 | Hardcover | $27.99 | 9781250786173 | Flatiron Books

CONVERSATION STARTERS

1. Olga and Prieto are highly-motivated, career-focused people who are invested in their communities. In what ways do the divergent trajectories of the two siblings reflect their different relationship to their hometown of Brooklyn, and the values of their society?

2. Family is an essential thread in this story and we see this through different lenses – whether it's Olga cunningly providing napkins for Mabel's wedding or whether it's Prieto rooting Olga on from the sidelines. Which of these moments resonated with you and how you show up for those in your own family? Why?

3. Mateo enters Olga's life and unapologetically discloses his own backstory. How does their romantic relationship change and influence some of the decisions Olga makes?

4. Evaluate Olga and Prieto's relationship with Blanca. How does their sense of self change as their relationship with their mother evolves throughout the novel?

5. The landfall of Hurricane Maria is crucial to the overarching plot, especially as we witness the lack of U.S. intervention in the aftermath. How does Gonzalez bring the discourse around aid and relief to the forefront of this novel through her characters?

6. How important was it for readers to hear Blanca's voice through her letters to her children? What did the letters reveal about Blanca's decisions when it came to her family? How did they make you feel about her choices?

7. How do the changes to the neighborhood where they grew up in affect Olga, Prieto and their friends and other family members differently? How does it feel unfair? How does Olga reconcile the transformation of her own life with the gentrification around her? How does it differ to Mateo?

8. Both Olga and Prieto are children of the diaspora, but they have different relationships to their communities and to Puerto Rico. Does one approach seem better than the other to you? Is it important to feel connected to one's roots?

9. In the beginning of the novel, Olga sees herself as more successful than Mabel. What do you think has shaped that notion of success and how do we feel that might have changed by the end?

THE PHONE BOOTH AT THE EDGE OF THE WORLD
Laura Imai Messina

When Yui loses both her mother and her daughter in the tsunami, she begins to mark the passage of time from that date onward: Everything is relative to March 11, 2011, the day the tsunami tore Japan apart, and when grief took hold of her life. Yui struggles to continue on, alone with her pain.

Then, one day she hears about a man who has an old disused telephone booth in his garden. There, those who have lost loved ones find the strength to speak to them and begin to come to terms with their grief. As news of the phone booth spreads, people travel to it from miles around.

Soon Yui makes her own pilgrimage to the phone booth, too. But once there she cannot bring herself to speak into the receiver. Instead she finds Takeshi, a bereaved husband whose own daughter has stopped talking in the wake of her mother's death.

Simultaneously heartbreaking and heartwarming, *The Phone Booth at the Edge of the World* is the signpost pointing to the healing that can come after.

"*An astonishment ... a quiet, contemplative, and gripping tale [that] provides a message of hope and endurance*" —**Christian Science Monitor**

"*A must-read ... a beautifully written book*" —**Kirkus**

"*Thoughtful and tender, full of small daily moments and acts of kindness, Messina's novel is a testament to the power of community (and a bit of whimsy) in moving forward after loss.*" —**Shelf Awareness**

ABOUT THE AUTHOR: **Laura Imai Messina** has made her home in Japan for the last 15 years and works between Tokyo and Kamakura, where she lives with her Japanese husband and two children. She has master's and doctorate degrees from Tokyo University. Translated from the Italian by Lucy Rand, *The Phone Booth at the Edge of the World* is Laura Imai Messina's English-language debut.

March 2021 | Hardcover | $25.00 | 9781419754302 | The Overlook Press

CONVERSATION STARTERS

1. What are some of the different ways the book portrays the relationship between parent and child? What does that relationship mean to Yui throughout the novel?

2. Throughout the book, almost everything is permeated by a kind of duality, that happiness can come with fear, grief can come with beauty, etc. What are some dualities in the book that spoke to you and how do they dictate they ways in which the characters approach the world?

3. How does wind define or enhance the most important moments in this story?

4. Did you want to know more about Susuki-san? About his background, education, or experience that led him to install the phone?

5. What does the man with the picture frame symbolize in the story?

6. A professional writer who plans to title his upcoming book The Age of Immortality suggests that his son drowned because of "bad luck." How does luck enter or affect any character's life in this novel?

7. How did you feel about the short chapters with lists and other details of daily life?

8. Why do you think Yui couldn't bring herself to talk on the phone?

9. What role does memory play in the book and what are some of the different perceptions of what it means to preserve things and people who have been lost?

10. Yui thinks to herself about how she might have cut herself into two: the world of the living and the world of the dead. How does this separation play out over the course of the novel?

11. How does the novel play with time? How does grief affect the way people perceive time in the book? Why do you think the author jumped from past to present to future in the book?

REELING
Sarah Stonich

What stage of grief is it when your grandmother's ghost keeps popping up on your electronic devices? Denial? For RayAnne that seems to be the stage for launching the second season of *Fishing!*—in New Zealand. Ready or not, she is taking public television's first all-women fishing talk show on the road, putting the cold Minnesota winter in the rearview mirror—which, it turns out, Gran is haunting, too.

After a challenging first season, and RayAnne's serendipitous ascension to host, there's a lot at stake. With camera-wielding twins Rongo and Rangi along as crew and tour guides, RayAnne and her indefatigable producer Cassi set out across New Zealand in search of noteworthy women who fish. Their stories, and a good dose of the country's history, are almost enough to take the edge off RayAnne's homesickness and grief, to say nothing of jetlag—and it doesn't hurt to discover a bird dog who fishes, an anti-fashionista, a pair of sisters fishing their way through recovery, and ... a Hobbit? Meanwhile, the romantic and family entanglements she left behind at home haven't exactly come untangled in her absence.

Those who met RayAnne in *Fishing!*, Sarah Stonich's first outing with the intrepid, accidental talk-show host, will encounter familiar and unexpected pleasures in her latest antics—and a story whose lighthearted surface and surprising depths will charm readers who now find her for the first time.

"This is a fun read, important and tender." —*Minneapolis Star Tribune*

ABOUT THE AUTHOR: **Sarah Stonich** is author of numerous books, including *Fishing!*, the first installment of RayAnne's adventures; *Vacationland* and *Laurentian Divide*, the first two volumes in her Northern Trilogy; *These Granite Islands*, which has been translated into seven languages and shortlisted for France's Grand Prix des Lectrices de Elle; and a memoir, *Shelter: Off the Grid in the Mostly Magnetic North*, all published by Minnesota. She lives on the Mississippi River in Minneapolis.

September 2021 | Paperback | $15.95 | 9781517908997 | University of Minnesota Press

CONVERSATION STARTERS

1. RayAnne's guests are odd and interesting. Which of them did you most relate to or connect with?

2. Should it matter that RayAnne is not a television 'professional'? She comes to her position only because the celebrity host walked off the show. Would you want to see more authentic or 'real' women on television and in the media?

3. What was the most surprising aspect of *Reeling*?

4. RayAnne is dealing with some sensitive issues, such as her father's battle with addiction and her grandmother's suicide. Are these topics given adequate consideration in the story?

5. If you found yourself on an elevator with RayAnne, what would you most want to talk about?

6. When was the last time you went fishing? Have you ever fished with friends?

7. A number of characters are of Māori ancestry. Did their portrayals seem realistic, or stereotyped? How far should an author go when writing about cultures that are not their own?

8. Can you think of an amazing or inspirational woman you'd like to see seated next to RayAnne for an interview?

9. RayAnne, alone on the Coromandel Peninsula has no Wi-Fi and no cell reception to speak of. Have you ever wished to be cut off in a such a way from the outside world, technology, or even loved ones?

10. Cassi and RayAnne take the show to New Zealand. If you could send them to a location of your choice, where would it be?

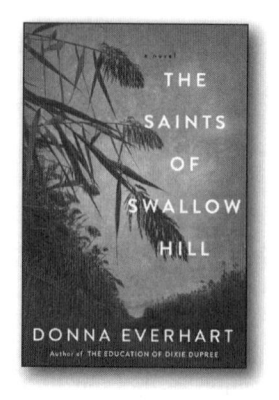

THE SAINTS OF SWALLOW HILL
Donna Everhart

Where the Crawdads Sing meets *The Four Winds* as award-winning author Donna Everhart immerses readers in a unique setting—a turpentine camp buried deep in the vast pine forests of Georgia during the Great Depression—for a captivating story of friendship, survival, and three vagabonds' intersecting lives.

During the Great Depression, destitute workers live and toil under terrible conditions in remote labor camps isolated throughout the expansive pine forests of the American South. As they harvest the pine gum that will be refined into turpentine, they are entirely dependent on greedy camp owners who provide food and housing at grossly inflated prices, creating an endless cycle of labor and debt. But for the most desperate among America's vast unemployed, these camps are often the last and only option.

This much is true for three individuals whose lives intersect in the deep woods of Georgia at the Swallow Hill turpentine camp in 1932. For Rae Lynn Cobb, a young woman disguised as a man, fleeing to Swallow Hill from North Carolina offers distance and anonymity from those who would wrongly imprison her for killing her kind though careless husband. For a charming bachelor named Del Reese, it's a place where backbreaking work might drown out memories of a recent trauma that's shaken him to his core.

But Swallow Hill is no easy haven. The squalid camp is ruled by a sadistic boss named Crow and the greedy commissary owner Otis Riddle, a man who takes out his frustrations on his wife, Cornelia. Del and "Ray Cobb" struggle to survive harsh, brutal conditions under the ever-watchful, narrow-minded Crow. As Rae Lynn forges a deeper friendship with both Del and Cornelia, she begins to envision a path out of the camp. But she will have to come to terms with her past, with all its pain and beauty, before she can open herself to a new life and seize the chance to begin again ...

ABOUT THE AUTHOR: **Donna Everhart** is the *USA Today* bestselling author of Southern fiction including *The Education of Dixie Dupree* and *The Moonshiner's Daughter*. She lives an hour away from where she was born and raised in Raleigh, North Carolina.

January 2022 | Paperback | $15.95 | 9781496733320 | Kensington Books

CONVERSATION STARTERS

1. What is your view Rae Lynn and Warren's marriage? Do you think it was a marriage of convenience, or love, or do you think it transformed over time?

2. When Del meets Elijah Sweeney, a.k.a. Crow, he senses the man is trouble and is immediately on guard. Have you ever met anyone who gave you the same sense? Did your instincts prove you right?

3. Swallow Hill was filled with dangers, not only from an environmental perspective, but with regard to some of the practices. How did the setting of the labor camp impact the story for you?

4. Keeping in mind the time frame, and the need for peo¬ple to be very self-sufficient, especially in remote areas, would/could you have done what Rae Lynn did for Warren after his accident?

5. A method of solitary confinement, known as a sweat box, is used in this story. How did it make you feel reading about the experiences of individuals placed inside them?

6. Crow shares his appreciation for the trees and doesn't want to see them ruined unnecessarily. Del admires this. Did Crow's view of nature change your perspective of him? How did you feel when you learned what happened to him?

7. Rae Lynn and Cornelia are both strong and brave women in their own way. What do you think was Rae Lynn's stron¬gest, bravest act? What about Cornelia's?

8. Both Del and Rae Lynn must confront their past in order to move forward. Are you aware of something from your own past that has held you back?

9. What does the title mean to you?

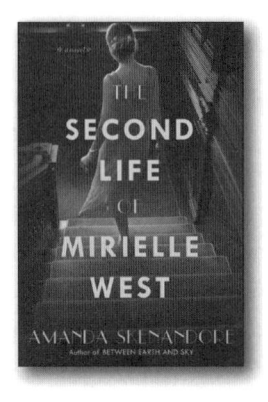

THE SECOND LIFE OF MIRIELLE WEST
Amanda Skenandore

Based on the little-known true story of America's only leper colony, *The Second Life of Mirielle West* by RUSA Award-winning author Amanda Skenandore brings vividly to life the Louisiana institution known as Carville, where thousands of people were stripped of their civil rights, branded as lepers, and forcibly quarantined throughout much of the 20th century.

For Mirielle West, a 1920's socialite married to a silent film star, the isolation and powerlessness of the Louisiana Leper Home is an unimaginable fall from her intoxicatingly glamorous life of bootlegged champagne and the star-studded parties of Hollywood's Golden Age. When a doctor notices a pale patch of skin on her hand, she's immediately branded a leper and carted hundreds of miles from home to Carville, taking a new name to spare her family and famous husband the shame that accompanies the disease.

At first she hopes her exile will be brief, but those sent to Carville are more prisoners than patients and their disease has no cure. Instead she must find community and purpose within its walls, struggling to redefine her self-worth while fighting an unchosen fate.

As a registered nurse, Amanda Skenandore's medical background adds layers of detail and authenticity to the experiences of patients and medical professionals Carville – the isolation, stigma, experimental treatments, and disparate community. A tale of repulsion, resilience, and the Roaring '20s, *The Second Life of Mirielle West* is also the story of a health crisis in America's past, made all the more poignant by the author's experiences during another, all-too-recent crisis.

ABOUT THE AUTHOR: **Amanda Skenandore** is a historical fiction writer and registered nurse. Her debut novel, *Between Earth and Sky*, was the winner of the American Library Association's RUSA Reading List for Best Historical Fiction Novel of the Year. She lives in Las Vegas, Nevada and can be found online at AmandaSkenandore.com.

July 2021 | Paperback | $15.95 | 9781496726513 | Kensington Books

CONVERSATION STARTERS

1. What assumptions did you have about leprosy before reading this book?

2. Patients at Carville fought for decades to promote the name Hansen's Disease over leprosy because of its strong, negative connotation. What power, if any, does language hold in erasing stigma?

3. Who was your favorite character in the story and why?

4. Mirielle begins the novel a broken, selfish woman. But through her experiences at Carville, she is able to grow and heal. Are there instances in your own life that may have been unwelcome but forced you nonetheless to change or grow?

5. How is Mirielle's approach to motherhood different at the beginning of the story than at the end? How does her approach compare to modern views of motherhood?

6. When Elena's infant is whisked away to the orphanage, Sister Verena tells Mirielle it's for the infant's own good. Do you agree?

7. The title of the novel implies something akin to a death, followed by a rebirth for Mirielle. What moment would you identify as her death? At what point did her new life begin? Was it a gradual process or an immediate change?

8. Frank believes that hope is as essential as medicine in surviving their disease. How big of a part does hope play in a struggle, particularly a struggle for survival?

9. For half a century, patients at Carville lived without the right to vote or marry or leave the confines of the hospital. Which of your freedoms would you most hate to give up?

10. In the aftermath of Carville and the tragic quarantining of Hansen's Disease patients, society continues to grapple with pandemic infectious disease (think of HIV and COVID-19). In what ways have we as a society progressed in dealing with these diseases? In what ways have we remained stagnant? Does stigma still play a role?

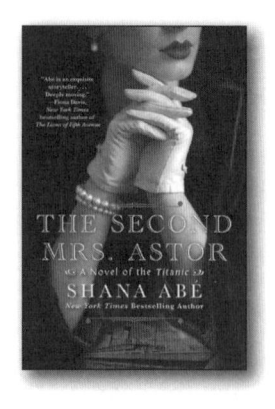

THE SECOND MRS. ASTOR
Shana Abé

In 1910, Jack Astor was one of the richest men in the world. Madeleine Force was a beautiful teenaged debutante suddenly thrust into fame simply for falling in love with a famous man nearly three decades her senior. From their scandalous courtship to their catastrophic honeymoon aboard the *Titanic*—a tragedy that transformed a pregnant Madeleine into the American Princess Diana of her time—their love story is now brought to life in this captivating work of historical fiction by *New York Times* bestselling novelist Shana Abé.

Madeleine Force is just 17 when she attracts the attention of John Jacob "Jack" Astor. Jack is dashing and industrious—a hero of the Spanish-American war, an inventor, and a canny businessman. Despite their 29-year age difference and the infamy of Jack's recent divorce, Madeleine falls headlong into love—and becomes the press's favorite target.

Marrying after a yearlong courtship that's constantly in the tabloids, the couple flees to Egypt. There they find a measure of peace, and they only decide to return when Madeleine is five months pregnant. They book their trip home aboard an opulent new ocean liner: the RMS *Titanic*.

Four months later, at the Astors' Fifth Avenue mansion, a widowed Madeleine gives birth to their son. In the wake of the disaster, the press has elevated her to the status of virtuous, tragic heroine. But Madeleine's most important decision still lies ahead: whether to accept the role assigned to her, or carve out her own remarkable path.

"Abé is an exquisite storyteller, gracefully transporting the reader from Newport to Egypt to the cold seas of the Atlantic." —**Fiona Davis**, *New York Times* **bestselling author of** *The Lions of Fifth Avenue*

"A gorgeous, phenomenal novel." —**Ellen Marie Wiseman**, *New York Times* **bestselling Author of** *The Orphan Collector*

ABOUT THE AUTHOR: **Shana Abé** is the award-winning, *New York Times*, *Wall Street Journal*, and *USA Today* bestselling author of more than a dozen novels. She lives in the mountains of Colorado and can be found online at ShanaAbe.com.

August 2021 | Paperback | $16.95 | 9781496732040 | Kensington Books

CONVERSATION STARTERS

1. At the beginning of the story, Madeleine is a sheltered seventeen-year-old socialite who has just graduated from finishing school. By the end of the novel, just two years later, her world is radically different. Do you think she handled the transition from relative obscurity to fame well? What would you have done differently?

2. Jack Astor was a man far more complex than the press portrayed, yet he was still incredibly wealthy, powerful, and renowned. Was he walking a morally ambiguous line by courting a teenaged girl nearly thirty years his junior? Do you believe he actually loved her, or was it just libido? Does the time period help excuse the age difference between them?

3. Their wedding ceremony took place just over a month after their engagement was publicly announced. Were Madeleine and Jack right to insist upon a swift, small wedding, instead of the huge social blowout that was more typical of their time and station? Do you think the primary motivator behind it all was their growing love for each other, or more a fear of the escalating scandal?

4. Madeleine's relationship with the press evolves over the course of the story. Do you think how she treated them was justified? Do you think how she was treated *by* them was justified?

5. As Titanic was sinking, no one in the Astor party had any way of knowing that Lifeboat Four was going to be one of the last to leave the ship. Should Madeleine have argued more forcibly to stay with Jack once it was clear he would not be allowed in the lifeboat? Or was she right to leave him behind?

6. Madeleine's interaction with Vincent was contentious from the beginning. As his future stepmother, should she have tried harder to befriend him? Or do you think it was always a hopeless cause?

7. Did Madeleine's grief force her to grow as a human being, as a soul, or did she perhaps shrink? Or both?

SMALL THINGS LIKE THESE
Claire Keegan

The landmark new novel from award-winning author Claire Keegan

It is 1985 in a small Irish town. During the weeks leading up to Christmas, Bill Furlong, a coal merchant and family man faces into his busiest season. Early one morning, while delivering an order to the local convent, Bill makes a discovery which forces him to confront both his past and the complicit silences of a town controlled by the church.

Already an international bestseller, *Small Things Like These* is a deeply affecting story of hope, quiet heroism, and empathy from one of our most critically celebrated and iconic writers.

"*Small Things Like These is a hypnotic and electrifying Irish tale that transcends country, transcends time. Claire Keegan's sentences make my heart pound and my knees buckle and I will always read everything she writes.*" —**Lily King, author of** *Writers & Lovers*

"*Claire Keegan creates scenes with astonishing clarity and lucidity. This is the story of what happened in Ireland, told with sympathy and emotional accuracy. From winter skies to the tiniest tick of speech to the baking of a Christmas cake, Claire Keegan makes her moments real—and then she makes them matter.*" —**Colm Tóibín, author of** *The Magician*

"*Makes you excited to discover everything its author has ever written. Absolutely beautiful.*" —**Douglas Stuart, author of** *Shuggie Bain*

ABOUT THE AUTHOR: **Claire Keegan** was raised on a farm in Ireland. Her stories have won numerous awards and are translated into more than twenty languages. *Antarctica* won the Rooney Prize for Irish Literature and was chosen as a *Los Angeles Times* Book of the Year. *Walk the Blue Fields* won the Edge Hill Prize for the finest collection of stories publishing in the British Isles. *Foster*, after wining the Davy Byrnes Award — then the world's richest prize for a story — was recently selected by *The Times* UK as one of the top 50 novels to be published in the 21st Century. Her stories have been published in the *New Yorker*, *Paris Review*, *Granta*, and *Best American Stories*. Keegan now holds the Briena Staunton Fellowship at Pembroke College, Cambridge.

November 2021 | Hardcover | $20.00 | 9780802158741 | Grove Atlantic

CONVERSATION STARTERS

1. Early in the novel, Furlong reflects on the movements of his family as they prepare for Christmas dinner. "Always it was the same ... they carried mechanically on, without pause, to the next job at hand. What would life be like, he wondered, if they were given time to think and to reflect over things?" How do the events that follow echo this meditation from Furlong?

2. Furlong provides for his family what he lacked as a child. Still, they are not rich. Why do you think Claire Keegan chose this man for her protagonist? What special insight do you think Furlong has that encourages his decision to return to the coal shed?

3. *Small Things Like These* occurs in just a few short weeks. Why do you think Claire Keegan chose to make the narrative so compact? How does the short sprint toward Christmas add to the climax of the novel?

4. After first meeting Sarah, Furlong sits alone in his truck before going "like a hypocrite, to mass." As her author note indicates, the Magdalene Laundries, where Sarah lives, were funded by both the Irish State and the Catholic Church. What role does religion play in this novel?

5. In many ways, Eileen balances Furlong. "You're soft-hearted, is all. Giving away what change is in your pocket," she says to him in bed, the night he returns from the Magdalene Laundries. Discuss her reaction to Furlong's prolonged anxiety. Do you agree with her idea that they ought to just "soldier on?"

6. In her note on the text, Claire Keegan, acknowledges the closing, in 1996, of the last Magdalene Laundry. At the end of her note, she quotes from the Proclamation of the Irish Republic: "The Irish Republic ... declares its resolve to pursue the happiness and prosperity of the whole nation and of all its parts, cherishing all of the children of the nation equally." Why do you think she juxtaposed these two facts? What resonance does this have with us today?

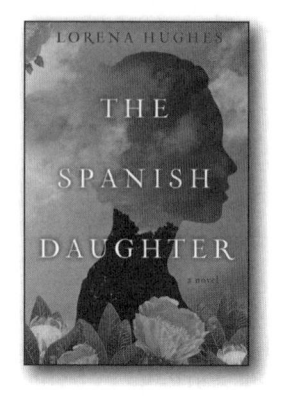

THE SPANISH DAUGHTER
Lorena Hughes

Set against the lush backdrop of 1920 Ecuador and inspired by the real-life history of the coastal town known as the birthplace of cacao, this captivating #OwnVoices novel from award-winning author Lorena Hughes tells the story of a resourceful young chocolatier who must impersonate a man in order to survive.

Puri inherited two things from her father: a passion for chocolate and a cacao plantation located in Ecuador. Bidding farewell to her native Spain and filled with hope for a new life after the devastation of WWI and a series of miscarriages, Puri sets out across the ocean with her husband. But someone is angered by her claim to the plantation ...

When a mercenary sent to murder her aboard the ship accidentally kills Cristóbal instead, Puri dons her husband's clothes and assumes his identity, hoping to stay safe while she learns the truth. Though freed from the rules that women are expected to follow, Puri confronts other challenges at the plantation—newfound siblings, hidden affairs, and her father's dark secrets. Then there are the dangers awakened by her attraction to an enigmatic man as she tries to learn the identity of an enemy who is still at large, threatening the future she is determined to claim.

ABOUT THE AUTHOR: **Lorena Hughes** is the award-winning author of *The Spanish Daughter* and *The Sisters of Alameda Street*. Born and raised in Ecuador, she moved to the United States when she was eighteen. Named one of 9 Rising Latina Authors You Don't Want to Miss by *Hip Latina*, she's the coordinator of the UNM Writers Conference. Lorena lives in Albuquerque, New Mexico and can be found online at Lorena-Hughes.com.

December 2021 | Paperback | $15.95 | 9781496736246 | Kensington Books

CONVERSATION STARTERS

1. Was Puri justified in deceiving her family? Why or why not?

2. Have you heard of real-life women cross-dressing to protect themselves or to perform activities that were reserved only for men? What are some examples? Do you think those women excelled in their fields?

3. Just like cacao beans transform into chocolate, Puri goes through a personal transformation after her experience of posing as a man. What are some of the things she discovers about herself and the opposite sex? How do her preconceptions regarding men and women change by the end of the novel?

4. How do you think Angélica, Catalina, Alberto, and Elisa would have reacted if Puri had presented herself as their sister when she first arrived? How about Martin?

5. Do you think Catalina was in love with Franco? What linked them together? How do you think her lie shaped the course of her life? Should she have told the truth at some point?

6. Martin tells Puri that his relationship with Angélica is complicated. Do you think they loved each other or just accustomed to one another? Do you think Puri is better suited for Martin? Why or why not? Do you see a future for them together?

7. Do you think Alberto had a true religious vocation despite his transgression? What are your thoughts regarding the Catholic Church's expectations for young men who enter priesthood?

8. Which of the sisters did you relate to the most? Was there a storyline or perspective that interested you the most?

9. Did you know anything about Ecuador before reading this novel? How has your perception of this country changed since you read it?

10. What were some of the cultural and historical details that surprised or interested you?

11. Family and jealousy are important themes in the novel. Puri longed for an intimate relationship with her father and later, with her siblings. Yet, she envies their closeness to her father. Similarly, her sisters experienced a desire to meet her, but were also jealous of her. Were you satisfied with the way their stories ended or would you prefer a different outcome for them?

THIS IS HAPPINESS: A NOVEL
Niall Williams

A profound and enchanting new novel from Booker Prize-longlisted author Niall Williams about the loves of our lives and the joys of reminiscing.

You don't see rain stop, but you sense it. You sense something has changed in the frequency you've been living and you hear the quietness you thought was silence get quieter still, and you raise your head so your eyes can make sense of what your ears have already told you, which at first is only: something has changed.

This is the story of all that was to follow: Christy's long-lost love and why he had come to Faha, Noel 'Noe' Crowe's own experiences falling in and out of love, and the endlessly postponed arrival of electricity--a development that, once complete, would leave behind a world that had not changed for centuries.

Niall Williams' latest novel is an intricately observed portrait of a community, its idiosyncrasies and its traditions, its paradoxes and its inanities, its failures and its triumphs. Luminous and otherworldly, and yet anchored with deep-running roots into the earthy and the everyday, *This Is Happiness* is about stories as the very stuff of life: the ways they make the texture and matter of our world, and the ways they write and rewrite us.

"Comic and poignant in equal measure." —**The New Yorker**

"This, truly, is happiness." —**Ron Charles**, *The Washington Post*

ABOUT THE AUTHOR: **Niall Williams** was born in Dublin in 1958. He studied English and French literature at University College Dublin before graduating with a Master's degree in Modern American Literature. He moved to New York in 1980 where he married Christine Breen. They moved to the cottage that Chris's grandfather had left eighty years before to find his life in America. His first four books were co-written with Chris and tell of their life together in Kiltumper in west Clare. Their latest book, *In Kiltumper*, was published by Bloomsbury, in August 2021.

December 2019 | Hardcover | $28.00 | 9781635574203 | Bloomsbury Publishing
August 2021 | Paperback | $17.00 | 9781635576313 | Bloomsbury Publishing

CONVERSATION STARTERS

1. How does Noe view the community he experienced in 1958? What has changed about the way we view community today? Where do you find community in your life?

2. What does the rain represent for the town? What does it mean that the rain has stopped?

3. If you could ask the author anything, what would it be?

4. Which scene has stuck with you the most?

5. Niall spends a lot of the novel describing the village of Faha. What were your favorite details?

6. Ron Charles wrote that the book "truly, is happiness" in his review. How would you describe your experience reading it?

7. *It had stopped raining.* What was the significance of this being the first line of the novel?

8. *This Is Happiness* is known for its beautiful, lyrical prose. Do you have a favorite passage?

9. Which character had the most impact on you? Noe, Christy, or the beloved Ganga?

10. How do you think the slower pace of this novel effects the storytelling?

11. Within the context of the novel, what do you believe is happiness?

12. *What does it matter what one old man was hoping one time?* Why does this question stay with you throughout the book? What does it mean?

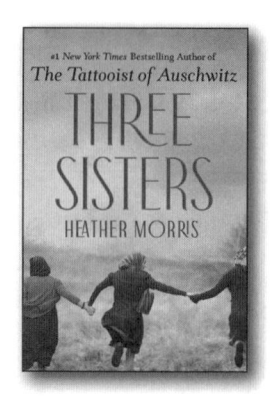

THREE SISTERS
Heather Morris

From Heather Morris, the *New York Times* bestselling author of the multi-million copy bestseller *The Tattooist of Auschwitz* and *Cilka's Journey*

Against all odds, three Slovakian sisters have survived years of imprisonment in the most notorious death camp in Nazi Germany: Auschwitz. Livia, Magda, and Cibi have clung together, nearly died from starvation and overwork, and the brutal whims of the guards in this place of horror. But now, the allies are closing in and the sisters have one last hurdle to face: the death march from Auschwitz, as the Nazis try to erase any evidence of the prisoners held there. Due to a last minute stroke of luck, the three of them are able to escape formation and hide in the woods for days before being rescued.

And this is where the story begins. From there, the three sisters travel to Israel, to their new home, but the battle for freedom takes on new forms. Livia, Magda, and Cibi must face the ghosts of their past–and some secrets that they have kept from each other–to find true peace and happiness.

Inspired by a true story, and with events that overlap with those of Lale, Gita, and Cilka, *The Three Sisters* will hold a place in readers' hearts and minds as they experience what true courage really is.

ABOUT THE AUTHOR: **Heather Morris** is a native of New Zealand, now resident in Australia. For several years, while working in a large public hospital in Melbourne, she studied and wrote screenplays, one of which was optioned by an Academy Award-winning screenwriter in the US. In 2003, Heather was introduced to an elderly gentleman who 'might just have a story worth telling'. The day she met Lale Sokolov changed both their lives. Their friendship grew and Lale embarked on a journey of self-scrutiny, entrusting the innermost details of his life during the Holocaust to her. Heather originally wrote Lale's story as a screenplay – which ranked high in international competitions – before reshaping it into her debut novel, *The Tattooist of Auschwitz*.

October 2021 | Hardcover | $28.99 | 9781250276896 | St. Martin's Press

CONVERSATION STARTERS

1. What do you think it was about these three sisters that meant they survived the Holocaust when so many others didn't? Was it luck or something else?

2. Why do you think the girls were so often treated better than other prisoners, by the block kapos and other guards, another fact that meant that they survived?

3. How important were relationships in the camps—between family, friends, and those in charge?

4. There is a sense that Magda felt guilt at not having been in the camp for as long as her sisters. Is this justified?

5. How do you think being in the camps shaped the people these three sisters became?

6. How did *Three Sisters* change your perceptions about the Holocaust in particular, and war in general? What implications does this book hold for our own time?

7. Why do you think the sisters chose to leave their home in Slovakia after the war and embark on a journey to Israel? Do you think they would have done this had it not been for their experiences in the Holocaust?

8. How do you think the sisters' experiences affected the relationships they formed after the Holocaust?

9. The scene in which the group of girls who have just survived the death march find an abandoned house and decide to take the dining table outside to eat is incredibly powerful. Why do you think they did this after everything they'd been through, rather than eating inside, and would you have done the same?

10. What was your overwhelming feeling when you finished the novel? Was it one of hope?

11. The sisters were barely older than children when they were taken to Auschwitz—Livia just fifteen. Do you think their youth gave them an advantage, or was the opposite the case?

12. Each of the sisters married a Holocaust survivor, with his own story of survival. Why do you think this might be?

13. Do you see the sisters as heroines or ordinary women?

THE TREES
Percival Everett

An uncanny literary thriller addressing the painful legacy of lynching in the US, by the author of *Telephone*, finalist for the Pulitzer Prize

Percival Everett's *The Trees* is a page-turner that opens with a series of brutal murders in the rural town of Money, Mississippi. When a pair of detectives from the Mississippi Bureau of Investigation arrive, they meet expected resistance from the local sheriff, his deputy, the coroner, and a string of racist White townsfolk. The murders present a puzzle, for at each crime scene there is a second dead body: that of a man who resembles Emmett Till.

The detectives suspect that these are killings of retribution, but soon discover that eerily similar murders are taking place all over the country. Something truly strange is afoot. As the bodies pile up, the MBI detectives seek answers from a local root doctor who has been documenting every lynching in the country for years, uncovering a history that refuses to be buried. In this bold, provocative book, Everett takes direct aim at racism and police violence, and does so in fast-paced style that ensures the reader can't look away. *The Trees* is an enormously powerful novel of lasting importance from an author with his finger on America's pulse.

"God bless Percival Everett, whose dozens of idiosyncratic books demonstrate a majestic indifference to literary trends, the market or his critics." —**The Wall Street Journal**

"Everett is an author who started his career off strong and just keeps getting better. [So Much Blue *is*] a generous, thrilling book by a man who might well be America's most under-recognized literary master." —**NPR.org**

"Like watching a skilled juggler execute a six-ball fountain, the experience of reading 'Telephone' is astonishing." —**Los Angeles Times**

ABOUT THE AUTHOR: **Percival Everett** is author to more than thirty books. He voted for Joe Biden.

September 2021 | Paperback | $16.00 | 9781644450642 | Graywolf Press

CONVERSATION STARTERS

1. *The Trees* employs caricature, satire, and historical fact. What is the relationship between stereotype and history? How do power dynamics change the impact and meaning of stereotypes?

2. Chester Hobsinger and Gertrude Penstock are mixed race and White-passing. How does this shape them and their roles in the book? How are they perceived by other characters and in what ways does this help or hinder them in meeting their goals?

3. The KKK stages a cross burning that goes wrong and mostly unnoticed. What does this say about the relationship between stupidity and violence, incompetence and innocence? How does that relationship change what is perceived as a threat?

4. What is the significance of Bluegum's, the dojo, and Black self-defense in *The Trees*?

5. *The Trees* is explicitly concerned with anti-Black police violence yet has three Black investigators as main characters. How does the author portray the tensions between policing and Blackness?

6. At the heart of *The Trees* is a massive archive of victims of anti-Black violence, many unnamed. What is the book saying about the relationship between memory and justice? Meanwhile, multiple Black characters have origin stories rooted in lynching. How does racist violence and racism shape families? What is included and omitted from family history?

7. *The Trees* is specifically concerned with America's anti-Blackness, yet it names the sites of violence that represent other marginalized identities as well. How do these types of violence relate? How is American anti-Blackness unique?

8. Damon Thruf begins by writing the name of every lynching victim in pencil with the goal to later erase them and "set them free." At the end of the novel, he is typing them instead. What do you think has changed?

9. How does humor diffuse or sharpen emotional responses to difficult material, historical or otherwise?

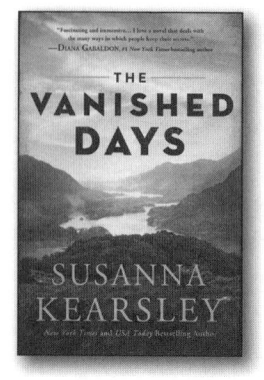

THE VANISHED DAYS
Susanna Kearsley

From international bestselling author Susanna Kearsley comes a historical tale of intrigue and revolution in Scotland, where the exile of King James brought plots, machinations, suspicion and untold bravery to light. An investigation of a young widow's secrets by a man who's far from objective, leads to a multi-layered tale of adventure, endurance, romance ... and the courage to hope.

In the autumn of 1707, old enemies from the Highlands to the Borders are finding common ground as they join to protest the new Union with England. At the same time, the French are preparing to launch an invasion to bring the young exiled Jacobite king back to Scotland to reclaim his throne, and in Edinburgh the streets are filled with discontent and danger.

Queen Anne's commissioners, seeking to calm the situation, have begun paying out money sent up from London to settle the losses and wages owed to those Scots who took part in the disastrous Darien expedition eight years earlier—an ill-fated venture that left Scotland all but bankrupt.

When the young widow of a Darien sailor comes forward to collect her husband's wages, her claim is challenged. One of the men assigned to investigate has only days to decide if she's honest, or if his own feelings are blinding him to the truth.

"I've loved every one of Susanna's books! Bedrock research and a butterfly's delicate touch with characters—historical fiction that sucks you in and won't let go!" —**Diana Gabaldon**, #1 *New York Times* **bestselling author of** *Outlander*

ABOUT THE AUTHOR: *New York Times* and *USA Today* bestselling author **Susanna Kearsley** is a former museum curator who loves restoring the lost voices of real people to the page. Her books, published in translation in more than 20 countries, and have won numerous awards. Susanna lives in Canada, by the shores of Lake Ontario.

October 2021 | Hardcover | $26.99 | 9781728249582 | Sourcebooks Landmark
October 2021 | Paperback | $16.99 | 9781492650164 | Sourcebooks Landmark

CONVERSATION STARTERS

1. Did you see the twist coming? Do you think the author played fair with her readers? Were there any particular clues that you spotted?

2. In the book, Adam tells us "if you've read this closely you will find I've sought to tell the truth." Did he? How do you feel about unreliable narrators? Do you have any favorite examples, in books or films?

3. In many dual-time stories, we have the benefit of a present-day narrator to interpret the past for us and explain what certain terms mean, but in this one, because both storylines are historical, we don't have that luxury. Did you have any trouble following the history because of this?

4. Do you think historical fiction is a valid and useful way to learn about history? Did you learn anything from this novel that you didn't know before about Scotland's (or America's) history?

5. Did it surprise you, on reading the author's note about the characters, to learn how many of the characters were real people? Does it change the way you look at a story to know that the characters actually lived?

6. Families—both the ones we're born into and the ones we create for ourselves—play a central part in this story. What different kinds of families did you find in this novel, and how do you feel they influenced the main characters?

7. The Browne family is not what you would call respectable, yet there are moments of great love and tenderness in their house. What is it that makes most of them, especially Barbara, sympathetic characters?

8. Henry says of his brother "Matthew was whatever ye had need of him to be, except dependable." Is that a fair judgment? Is there a moment that shows us he has changed?

9. Why do you think Adam and Lily chose America as the place to start their new life together? What did it offer them that Scotland at that time did not?

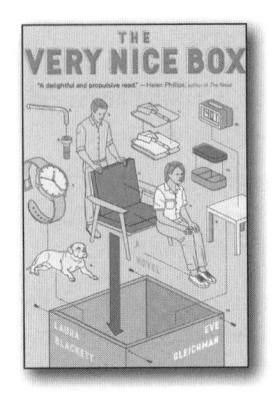

THE VERY NICE BOX
Eve Gleichman & Laura Blackett

Corporate satire meets rom-com in this darkly funny, suspenseful debut – with a shocking twist

For fans of *Elinor Oliphant Is Completely Fine* and *Severance*: an offbeat, wryly funny debut novel that follows an eccentric product engineer who works for a hip furniture company where sweeping corporate change lands her under the purview of a startlingly charismatic boss who seems determined to get close to her at all costs.

"A quirky, deeply satisfying, whip-smart debut that critiques corporate culture and male entitlement while also offering a heartfelt look at how to work through grief. Meticulously constructed and truly original—I inhaled it." —**Jami Attenberg, author of** *All This Could Be Yours*

"Eve Gleichman and Laura Blackett have managed to write a literary page-turner that is full of heart and scathing social critique, not to mention a surprise ending to rival those of my favorite mysteries. I absolutely devoured it." —**Melissa Febos, author of** *Girlhood*

"A satire of contemporary corporate culture. An exploration of how vulnerable we become in grief. A surprising romance. A cautionary tale. Somehow The Very Nice Box *manages to be all of the above. Eve Gleichman and Laura Blackett have a wicked sense of humor and a keen view on our current moment. This is a delightful and propulsive read.*" —**Helen Phillips, author of** *The Need*

ABOUT THE AUTHORS: **Eve Gleichman's** short stories have appeared in the *Kenyon Review*, the *Harvard Review*, *BOMB Daily*, and elsewhere. Eve is a graduate of Brooklyn College's Fiction MFA Program and lives in Brooklyn.

Laura Blackett is a woodworker and writer based in Brooklyn.

July 2021 | Hardcover | $25.00 | 9780358540113 | Mariner Books

CONVERSATION STARTERS

1. Consider how the authors employ satire. What does the opening of the story reveal about STÄDA and its culture? As Ava stands in the Imagination Room for the announcement of Karl's departure, she wonders "Am I in a cult?" (13). How would you answer her question?

2. What are Mat's first interactions with Ava like and what are her first impressions of him? Why does Ava accept a ride home from Mat even though it was "the last thing [she] wanted" (24)? Were you surprised when she agreed to meet Mat at the dog park the following day?

3. How does STÄDA "demand" the so-called "self-care" of its employees? What is problematic about this? What does this say about the true nature of self-care and wellness and how they can best be cultivated?

4. When Mat tells Ava about an email from Judith in which she chided him for being five minutes late to his job interview, Ava thinks "men got to be this way ... constantly in the midst of forgiving themselves" (48). What do you think she meant by this? Where else does the book offer thoughts on male entitlement?

5. Evaluate the symbolism of the Very Nice Box. Why did Ava feel so passionate about this particular project? What do you think that the box represents for her? Why do you think the book was named after this object? How does it reflect or refer readers back to the major themes and motifs of the book?

6. How does the book provide a counterpoint to the characterization of the Vandals? Why does a member of this group tell a reporter that it is ironic that STÄDA sees itself as the victim? Who are the Vandals revealed to be at the book's conclusion and how does this tie in with contemporary conversations about activists and their portrayal in the media?

7. How do the authors create suspense within the story and how does this contribute to a conversation about the themes of trust and intuition? What were some of the red flags that Ava ignored? What made her particularly vulnerable to Mat's predatory behavior? What does the book ultimately suggest about who one should make oneself vulnerable to and how can people make good choices in this area?

8. What is it that Mat and Ava ultimately have in common? At the end of the novel, how has she been changed by her experience and what steps does she say that she wants to take in order to begin a true process of healing?

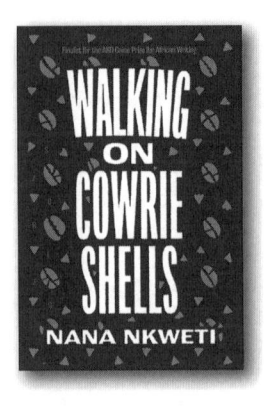

WALKING ON COWRIE SHELLS: STORIES
Nana Nkweti

A "boisterous and high-spirited debut" (*Kirkus* starred review) "that enthralls the reader through their every twist and turn" (*Publishers Weekly* starred review)

In her powerful debut story collection, Nana Nkweti's virtuosity is on full display as she mixes deft realism with clever inversions of genre. In the Caine Prize finalist story "It Takes a Village, Some Say," she skewers racial prejudice and the practice of international adoption, delivering a sly tale about a teenage girl who leverages her adoptive parents to fast-track her fortunes. In "The Devil Is a Liar" a pregnant pastor's wife struggles with the collision of Western Christianity and her mother's traditional Cameroonian belief system as she worries about her unborn child.

In other stories, Nkweti vaults past realism, upending genre expectations in a satirical romp about a jaded PR professional trying to spin a zombie outbreak in West Africa, and in a mermaid tale about a Mami Wata who forgoes her power by remaining faithful to a fisherman she loves. In between these two ends of the spectrum there's everything from an aspiring graphic novelist at a comic con, to a murder investigation driven by statistics, to a story organized by the changing hairstyles of the main character.

Pulling from mystery, horror, realism, myth, and graphic novels, Nkweti showcases the complexity and vibrance of characters whose lives span Cameroonian and American cultures.

"[Walking on Cowrie Shells] *revels in variety—of character, style, and even genre … Lively and fast-paced, funny and tragic, these stories refuse a singular African experience in favor of a vivid plurality.*" —**The New Yorker**

ABOUT THE AUTHOR: **Nana Nkweti** is a Caine Prize finalist and alumna of the Iowa Writers' Workshop. Her work has garnered fellowships from MacDowell, Kimbilio, Ucross, and the Wurlitzer Foundation, among others. She is a professor of English at the University of Alabama.

June 2021 | Paperback | $24.95 | 9781644450543 | Graywolf Press

CONVERSATION STARTERS

1. The stories in *Walking on Cowrie Shells* create worlds unto themselves. Name three examples of how Nkweti uses different storytelling techniques—such as voice, perspective, suspense, humor—to create different effects for the reader.

2. Cameroonian American characters in the collection must grapple at times with not easily fitting into either culture. How does this play out for them? How do they carve out places for themselves?

3. The Maroua Market, referred to in "Night Becomes Us," was hit by a suicide bombing in 2015. How does this knowledge affect the reading of this story?

4. The eerie and satirical tale "It Just Kills You Inside" revolves around a zombie outbreak in Cameroon's Lake Nyos. Though it was written before, how is the experience of reading this story different in light of the COVID-19 pandemic?

5. Why might the romantic relationship in "The Living Infinite" be considered unconventional? Does this couple bring to mind any other powerful matches in literature, mythology, or popular culture?

6. The cultural myth of monolithic Blackness often creates real pressure to oversimplify Blackness to a few known dimensions. How do the narratives in Walking on Cowrie Shells complicate this myth and offer varying representations of Blackness? In which moments is this tension most extreme?

7. Women take center stage in these narratives—not just the young female protagonists, but their aunties, their little sisters, their frenemies. What are a few of the myriad ways these stories explore the complexities of African womanhood? In what ways do these characters push against boundaries and expectations?

8. Nkweti chooses not to translate any of the non-English words. What effect does this have for the reader who understands these languages? What effect does this have for those who do not?

9. The title comes from page 170 when Jennifer says "She felt like a counterfeit African, felt the unworthiness of the maid's child tiptoeing through the servants' entrance, lightly, quietly, like she was walking on cowrie shells." How does that title phrase relate to Jennifer's experience in this story? How does it relate to the collection as a whole?

ReadingGroupChoices.com

THE WAR NURSE
Tracey Enerson Wood

Based on a true story, *The War Nurse* is a sweeping historical novel by *USA Today* bestselling author Tracey Enerson Wood that takes readers on an unforgettable journey through WWI France.

Superintendent of Nurses Julia Stimson must recruit sixty-four nurses to relieve the battle-worn British, months before American troops are ready to be deployed. She knows that the young nurses serving near the front lines of will face a challenging situation, but nothing could have prepared her for the chaos that awaits when they arrive at British Base Hospital 12 in Rouen, France. The primitive conditions, a convoluted, ineffective system, and horrific battle wounds are enough to discourage the most hardened nurses, and Julia can do nothing but lead by example—even as the military doctors undermine her authority and make her question her very place in the hospital tent.

When trainloads of soldiers stricken by a mysterious respiratory illness arrive one after the other, overwhelming the hospital's limited resources, and threatening the health of her staff, Julia faces an unthinkable choice—to step outside the bounds of her profession and risk the career she has fought so hard for, or to watch the people she cares for most die in her arms.

"Through careful research, this book shows the incredible bravery and compassion of women who find themselves in extraordinary situations." —**Julia Kelly, international bestselling author of** *The Last Garden in England*

"A rich, gripping history of one woman's lifelong battle against systemic prejudice." —**Stewart O'Nan, award-winning author of** *The Good Wife*

"Once again, Tracey Enerson Wood, with her impeccable research and evocative prose, kept me glued to the page. Wood has a talent for bringing strong, yet lesser-known women from history, to life." —**Linda Rosen, author of** *The Disharmony of Silence*

"A riveting and surprisingly timely story of courage, sacrifice, and friendship forged at the front lines." —**Kelly Mustian, author of** *The Girls in the Stilt House*

ABOUT THE AUTHOR: **Tracey Enerson Wood** is a published playwright whose family is steeped in military tradition. This is her second novel, following *The Engineer's Wife*.

July 2021 | Hardcover | $26.99 | 9781492698166 | Sourcebooks Landmark
March 2022 | Paperback | $16.99 | 9781728242873 | Sourcebooks Landmark

CONVERSATION STARTERS

1. How much did you know about nursing (particularly World War I-era nursing) before reading this book? What was the most surprising thing you learned?

2. If you were told that your entire workplace was uprooting to support a war effort, what would your first reaction be? Did Julia have a real choice when it came to shipping out?

3. Both Julia and the doctors she assists can be territorial about their authority. How does this affect their working dynamics? Are there any consequences for the patients the team treats?

4. Julia and Dr. Murphy discuss the ethical and procedural challenges of authorizing nurses to perform lifesaving procedures on their own. Compare the benefits and drawbacks of strictly following protocol to the consequences of a nurse performing whatever procedures she feels are best.

5. Julia hesitates in her relationship with Fred, not wanting to feed the rumor mill. How does outside opinion influence relationships? Compare the rumor mill of Base Hospital 21 to today's social media. How do their relative positions affect their willingness to "let the chips fall where they may" when they begin seeing each other more seriously?

6. What did you think of Julia's choice to keep her skin condition a secret? Do you think she was right to fear dismissal? What were the consequences of her decision?

7. How does the 1918 Spanish flu outbreak compare to the 2020 novel coronavirus? Are there lessons that can be learned from the way Julia and her nurses battle their pandemic?

8. Did Julia do the right thing by violating protocol to operate on Private Dempsey? What would you have done in her place?

9. What did you think of the final scene of the book? What do you think is next for Julie and Fred?

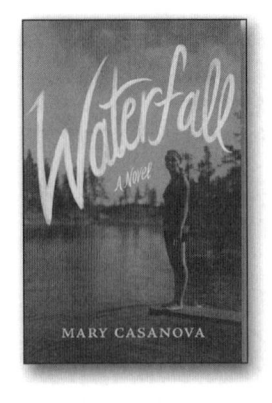

WATERFALL
Mary Casanova

In her third Rainy Lake historical drama, Mary Casanova takes us back to pristine and rugged northern Minnesota. It's 1922, women have won the right to vote, and Trinity Baird is of age. But at 21, and after nearly two years at Oak Hills Asylum, she returns to her family's island summer home with her self-confidence in tatters and her mind seared by haunting memories. Her parents are oblivious to what they have put her through and instead watch their daughter for the least sign of defiance. Trinity struggles to be the "respectable" young woman her parents (especially her mother) demand, so that she can return to her independent life studying art and painting in Paris. She never wants to go back to Oak Hills, where they "treat" *hysterical*, i.e., unconventional, young women.

Informed by historical figures, by the burgeoning growth of women's rights in the early twentieth century, and the complicated issue of mental illness and how "difficult" women were silenced, *Waterfall* offers a compelling story of an inspired, ambitious, and soulful young woman's fight to find her way.

"A thoughtful, beautifully written, and deeply satisfying read, this book shows that one can go over the waterfall and still survive." —**Mary Logue, author of** *The Streel* **and the Claire Watkins mystery series**

"With its glorious setting contrasting with the realities of the era, Waterfall *details darker aspects of the Roaring Twenties, but also celebrates the reemergence of an individual spirit."* —*ForeWord Reviews*

"A refreshing and satisfying read." —*Minneapolis Star Tribune*

ABOUT THE AUTHOR: **Mary Casanova** is author of thirty-nine books, ranging from picture books to historical fiction, including *Hush, Hush Forest*; *Frozen*; and *Ice-Out*, published by Minnesota. Her numerous awards include an American Library Association "Notable," Aesop Accolades from the American Folklore Society, a Parent's Choice Gold Award, Booklist Editor's Choice, as well as two Minnesota Book Awards.

April 2021 | Hardcover | $22.95 | 9781517901745 | University of Minnesota Press

CONVERSATION STARTERS

1. Consider and discuss a 'woman's place' in society in the early 20th century. How does Trinity push the boundaries and demonstrate courage and determination?

2. What are the differences between the diagnosis and treatment of mental illness then and now?

3. How does Trinity's family wealth act as a contributor to her difficulties? To her successes?

4. This being a story of self-realization, discuss the changes you see in Trinity as the novel unfolds. What precipitates these changes?

5. We see wealth and privilege portrayed alongside poverty and servitude. In what instances do you share Trinity's discomfort and unease? Why?

6. Consider the environmental concerns of Ernest Oberholtzer/Victor Guttenberg. How were his ideas shaped by his relationship with American Indians?

7. What are Trinity's main challenges? How does she overcome them?

8. Values drive behavior. Therefore, what are the underpinning values of the novel? What are the driving values of various characters?

9. If a romantic relationship continued between Max and Trinity, what kind of hardships and choices might they encounter?

10. Regarding Trinity's asylum doctor: How were his role and counsel instrumental in her 'recovery'?

11. Trinity is a young woman ahead of her time in many ways. How does that impact her relationships with her mother and sister? With her fellow Asylum inmates? With Victor, Henry, and Max?

NONFICTION

DANCING WITH THE OCTOPUS: A MEMOIR OF A CRIME
Debora Harding

Named one of the Best True Crime Books by *Marie Claire*, *Dancing with the Octopus* is a harrowing, redemptive and profoundly inspiring memoir of childhood trauma and its long reach into adulthood.

One Omaha winter day in November 1978, when Debora Harding was just fourteen, she was abducted at knifepoint from a church parking lot. She was thrown into a van, assaulted, held for ransom, and then left to die as an ice storm descended over the city.

Debora survived. She identified her attacker to the police and then returned to her teenage life in a dysfunctional home where she was expected to simply move on. Denial became the family coping strategy offered by her fun-loving, conflicted father and her cruelly resentful mother.

It wasn't until decades later - when beset by the symptoms of PTSD- that Debora undertook a radical project: she met her childhood attacker face-to-face in prison and began to reconsider and reimagine his complex story. This was a quest for the truth that would threaten the lie at the heart of her family and with it the sacred bond that once saved her.

Dexterously shifting between the past and present, Debora Harding untangles the incident of her kidnapping and escape from unexpected angles, offering a vivid, intimate portrait of one family's disintegration in the 1970s Midwest.

Written with dark humor and the pacing of a thriller, *Dancing with the Octopus* is a literary tour de force and a groundbreaking narrative of reckoning, recovery, and the inexhaustible strength it takes to survive.

"This book is personal, deeply and bravely thoughtful, and creatively expressed ... It can serve as a tool for the politically engaged." —**New York Journal of Books**

ABOUT THE AUTHOR: **Debora Harding** grew up in the Midwest and then spent three decades immersed in Washington politics. While cycling across America she met her English husband. She is mother of two children and is now a full-time writer and activist. She splits her time between the United States and Great Britain

September 2021 | Paperback | $17.00 | 9781635577846 | Bloomsbury

CONVERSATION STARTERS

1. The memoir takes place in Nebraska, Iowa, West Virginia, and England, among other locations. What's the importance of *place* in Harding's story? How has geography shaped her life, and how has she made homes, for herself and loved ones, in different settings?

2. Harding details years of abuse at the hands of her mother (Kathleen Cackler). How did the members of the author's family cope with this abuse? What adaptations did they develop to shield themselves and comfort others?

3. Harding mentions, in her epilogue, that she wants to "portray 'victims' realistically" (372). Before, during, and after the attack, Harding demonstrates remarkable resilience and agency. What does Harding gain from recalling, corroborating, and writing down her experience?

4. Part of Harding's resilience is her ability to accept the help of others. How does her husband Thomas support her? What tools and advice does Dr. H provide?

5. Discuss the role race plays in the narrative. How does Harding work serious considerations of race into the story of her attack and its aftermath? How does Charles Goodwin understand race to have informed his own experiences?

6. Like Charles (Mr. K), Harding's mother has had significant challenges in life. How does Kathleen explain away, or justify, her abuse of her children and husband? How does Harding balance empathy for Kathleen with her own traumatic memories of her mother's violence?

7. What forms of support does Harding find in the Omaha community, in the immediate aftermath of her kidnapping and assault? And whom does she rely on when she returns to Omaha as an adult?

8. How is the "dancing octopus" introduced in the narrative? Whose creation is it? And when Harding sees a real octopus, years later, what does she feel? With whom does she share this second experience?

9. Jim eventually reveals his own traumatic memories to Harding. What are these memories, and how does he tell his story? What are the coping mechanisms and kinds of fellowship--productive and unproductive--Jim turns to as he grows older?

10. Why do you think Harding chose to use this narrative structure? What insights were made possible for the reader due to the structure?

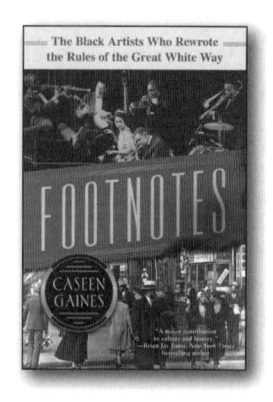

FOOTNOTES: THE BLACK ARTISTS WHO REWROTE THE RULES OF THE GREAT WHITE WAY
Caseen Gaines

The triumphant story of how an all-Black Broadway cast and crew changed musical theatre—and the world—forever.

If *Hamilton*, *Rent*, or *West Side Story* captured your heart, you'll love this in-depth look into the rise of the 1921 Broadway hit, *Shuffle Along*, the first all-Black musical to succeed on Broadway. No one was sure if America was ready for a show featuring nuanced, thoughtful portrayals of Black characters—and the potential fallout was terrifying. But from the first jazzy, syncopated beats of composers Noble Sissle and Eubie Blake, New York audiences fell head over heels.

Footnotes is the story of how Sissle and Blake, along with comedians Flournoy Miller and Aubrey Lyles, overcame poverty, racism, and violence to harness the energy of the Harlem Renaissance and produce a runaway Broadway hit that launched the careers of many of the twentieth century's most beloved Black performers. Born in the shadow of slavery and establishing their careers at a time of increasing demands for racial justice and representation for people of color, they broke down innumerable barriers between Black and white communities at a crucial point in our history.

Caseen Gaines leads readers through the glitz and glamour of New York City during the Roaring Twenties to reveal the revolutionary impact one show had on generations of Americans, and how its legacy continues to resonate today.

"Exuberant and thoroughly captivating book ... Gaines is in full command of the material he has fastidiously researched and assembled." — **The New York Times**

"Absorbing." —**Wall Street Journal**

ABOUT THE AUTHOR: **Caseen Gaines** has written for Rolling Stone, Vanity Fair, and NY Magazine. He holds an MA from Rutgers Uni in American Studies, focusing on racial representations in popular culture.

May 2021 | Hardcover | $26.99 | 9781492688815 | Sourcebooks
October 2022 | Paperback | $16.99 | 9781728259390 | Sourcebooks

CONVERSATION STARTERS

1. In the opening of the book, Sissle, Miller, and Lyles brace for the worst during Shuffle Along's most sincere love song. Why were they so afraid of the fallout from that particular scene?

2. In describing Miller's childhood, Gaines draws attention to the relationship between economic class and racism. How would you describe that relationship? What are some ways in which race and class intersect throughout the narrative?

3. Diverse racial representation has a marked impact on audiences, but what effect does it have on future productions?

4. Blake's parents disagreed about whether to talk about their pasts. Blake's mother would never even admit that she had been enslaved, while his father thought discussing slavery was crucial. Who did you agree with and why?

5. When the James Reese Europe's Society Orchestra is served dishwater instead of the meal they were promised, Blake observes that "Jim Europe didn't get where he is with the white folks by complainin'." How does this capture the tenuous balance the performers were trying to strike between large-scale success and respect?

6. Describe Jim Europe's impact on Noble Sissle. How did Europe's example guide Sissle in advancing his career and highlighting the artistry of other Black performers?

7. Shuffle Along was celebrated for introducing Black women to the stage but earns a reputation for rejecting or sidelining chorus girls for being "too dark." Were the show's creators wrong for casting based on skin color? How does colorism compare to racism more generally?

8. Miller and Lyles thought that it was unfair that Blake and Sissle were making more money from the show and its music. Did you think Miller and Lyles were entitled to any portion of the royalties from Shuffle Along's sheet music?

9. In their later ventures, Sissle and Blake were challenged by (white) critics who thought their shows had "too much 'art' and not enough Africa." How did they handle this criticism? What would you have done in their position?

10. In your opinion, what is Shuffle Along's most lasting impact?

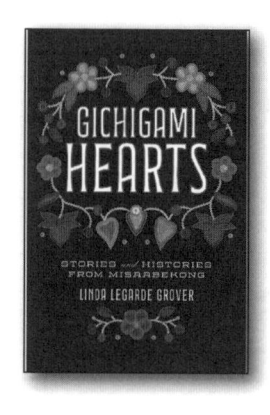

GICHIGAMI HEARTS: STORIES AND HISTORIES FROM MISAABEKONG
Linda LeGarde Grover

Long before there was a Duluth, Minnesota, the massive outcropping that divides the city emerged from the ridge of gabbro rock running along the westward shore of Lake Superior. A great westward migration carried the Ojibwe people to this place, the Point of Rocks. Against this backdrop— Misaabekong, the place of the giants—the lives chronicled in Linda LeGarde Grover's book unfold, some in myth, some in long-ago times, some in an imagined present, and some in the author's family history, all with a deep, tenacious bond to the land, one another, and the Ojibwe culture. Within the larger history, Grover tells the story of her ancestors' arrival in Duluth over two hundred years ago. Blending the seen and unseen, the old and the new, the amusing and the tragic and the hauntingly familiar, this lyrical work encapsulates a way of life forever vibrant at the Point of Rocks.

"With compelling stories of sacred places, beloved people, myths, legends, and treasured memories, Gichigami Hearts *is a moving tribute to the Ojibwe past."* —**Carolyn Holbrook, author of** *Tell Me Your Names and I Will Testify*

"Linda LeGarde Grover weaves a generational history of a sacredness inseparable from place, of the unbroken chain of Anishinaabe existence in Missabekong. Her powerful prose and ethereal poetry wash over the pages like waves along the shore of Lake Superior, revealing a strength of survival that goes beyond memory and reminding us to watch, listen, and breathe."
—**Gwen Westerman, Minnesota State University, Mankato**

ABOUT THE AUTHOR: **Linda LeGarde Grover** is professor of American Indian studies at the University of Minnesota Duluth and a member of the Bois Forte Band of Ojibwe. She is author of several award-winning books, including *The Road Back to Sweetgrass*, *Onigamiising: Seasons of an Ojibwe Year*, and *In the Night of Memory*, all from Minnesota, as well as *The Dance Boots* and *The Sky Watched*.

October 2021 | Paperback | $14.95 | 9781517911935 | University of Minnesota Press

CONVERSATION STARTERS

1. The landscapes and natural surroundings of northeastern Minnesota play key roles in many events described in *Gichigami Hearts*. In your own experience and as a reader, how does this bring to mind a similar integration of the backdrop of the physical world and that sense of time and place?

2. The epigraph in *Gichigami Hearts* is an excerpt from *The Dance Boots*, Grover's 2010 short fiction collection, quoting the fictional Artense Gallette imagining the reuniting of Grover's grandfather Elias with his true love, Victoria, after death. What might be some examples of love—lost, found, unrequited, reunited—that connect the stories and poems of *Gichigami Hearts*?

3. In reading this collection, we encounter interweavings between Ojibwe traditional beliefs and stories and the history of Duluth and its terrain and landmarks—the Point of Rocks, hills, and Gichigami (Lake Superior). What do you think are some of the reasons this combination has been important to the Ojibwe people of that region?

4. The formal schooling education of American Indian children in the Indian boarding school system casts a long shadow over the history of Linda's family, as well as probably every other Native family in America. What might be some of the ways in which families and family life were affected, and do you think that those effects continue in Native families and communities today?

5. In "Life Among the Italians" Grover suggests that the fondness the Italian grandfather had for the LeGarde children may have been because of his general love for children, the LeGarde children's physical appearance, and that the prejudices the Italian people experienced might have had parallels to those of the Indians. What might some of these experiences have been? Have you heard about or seen similar situations or histories?

6. What do you think are some of the complicated legacies that Elias and the other ancestors in *Gichigami Hearts* left for their descendants and extended families, for the Anishinaabe/Ojibwe people, for all of us?

THE KISSING BUG: A TRUE STORY OF A FAMILY, AN INSECT, AND A NATION'S NEGLECT OF A DEADLY DISEASE
Daisy Hernández

Who does the United States take care of, and who does it leave behind? A necessary investigation of infectious disease, poverty, racism, and for-profit healthcare—and the harm caused by decades of neglect.

Growing up in a New Jersey factory town in the 1980s, Daisy Hernández believed that her aunt had become deathly ill from eating an apple. No one in her family, in either the United States or Colombia, spoke of infectious diseases. Even into her thirties, she only knew that her aunt had died of Chagas, a rare and devastating illness that affects the heart and digestive system. But as Hernández dug deeper, she discovered that Chagas—or the kissing bug disease—is more prevalent in the United States than the Zika virus.

After her aunt's death, Hernández began searching for answers. Crisscrossing the country, she interviewed patients, doctors, epidemiologists, and even veterinarians with the Department of Defense. She learned that in the United States more than three hundred thousand people in the Latinx community have Chagas, and that outside of Latin America, this is the only country with the native insects—the "kissing bugs"—that carry the Chagas parasite.

Through unsparing, gripping, and humane portraits, Hernández chronicles a story vast in scope and urgent in its implications, exposing how poverty, racism, and public policies have conspired to keep this disease hidden. A riveting investigation into racial politics and for-profit healthcare in the United States, *The Kissing Bug* reveals the intimate history of a marginalized disease and connects us to the lives at the center of it all.

"An absolutely essential perspective on global migration, poverty, and pandemics." —**Amy Stewart, author of** *Wicked Bugs*

ABOUT THE AUTHOR: **Daisy Hernández** is a former reporter for *The New York Times* and has written for *National Geographic*, NPR's *All Things Considered* and *Code Switch*, *The Atlantic*, *Slate*, and *Guernica*. Hernández is the author of the award-winning memoir *A Cup of Water Under My Bed*.

June 2021 | Hardcover | $27.95 | 9781951142520 | TinHouse

CONVERSATION STARTERS

1. Had you heard of Chagas disease before reading this book? Were there things you learned about that surprised you?

2. Danielle Ofri calls *The Kissing Bug* "a deft mix of family archaeology, parasite detective story, and American reckoning." In a few words, how would you characterize the book?

3. How was the book structured? How did this affect the story and your appreciation of the book?

4. Author Daisy Hernández begins the narrative in childhood, with a scene of her aunt in the hospital. Why do you think she chose to start in this way?

5. "While other girls my age were taught to fear rabid dogs and horrible men," says Hernández, "I learned to be terrified of an insect the size of my fingernail, an insect that could kill a woman's heart. And as with all private mythologies, this one began before my mother was born." Growing up, was there anything that your family's particular history taught you to fear?

6. Says Hernández: "The corazón, the heart, is an accordion … The kissing bug disease tampers with this music." How does she use metaphor and other techniques here and elsewhere to help explain complicated medical and scientific concepts? Why might she, at times, be writing in this way, rather than using more technical terminology?

7. Of all the patients Hernández interviews in the book, was there one you connected with most? Why do you think it was important to Hernández to include so many individual stories?

8. Angie Cruz says that "The question *The Kissing Bug* investigates is timely: Who does the United States take care of, and who does it leave behind?" After reading the book, how would you answer this question?

9. In your opinion, could more be done to educate the American public about Chagas disease? What kinds of steps might be taken?

10. If you could recommend this book to anyone in the world, who would you share it with? Who do you think most needs to read these pages?

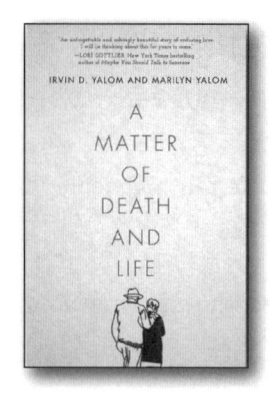

A MATTER OF DEATH AND LIFE
Irvin D. Yalom and Marilyn Yalom

Internationally acclaimed psychiatrist and author Irvin Yalom devoted his career to counseling those suffering from anxiety and grief. But never had he faced the need to counsel himself until his wife, esteemed feminist author Marilyn Yalom, was diagnosed with cancer. In *A Matter of Death and Life*, Marilyn and Irv share how they took on profound new struggles: Marilyn to die a good death, Irv to live on without her.

In alternating accounts of their last months together and Irv's first months alone, they offer us a rare window into facing mortality and coping with the loss of one's beloved. The Yaloms had numerous blessings—a loving family, a Palo Alto home under a magnificent valley oak, a large circle of friends, avid readers around the world, and a long, fulfilling marriage—but they faced death as we all do. With the wisdom of those who have thought deeply, and the familiar warmth of teenage sweethearts who've grown up together, they investigate universal questions of intimacy, love, and grief.

Informed by two lifetimes of experience, *A Matter of Death and Life* is an openhearted offering to anyone seeking support, solace, and a meaningful life.

"It will inspire you and perhaps move you to look differently at your life—it did that for me." —**Abraham Verghese, author of** *Cutting for Stone*

ABOUT THE AUTHORS: **Irvin D. Yalom**, emeritus professor of psychiatry at Stanford University, is the author of internationally bestselling books, including *Love's Executioner*, *The Gift of Therapy*, *Becoming Myself*, and *When Nietzsche Wept*.

Marilyn Yalom's books include classics of cultural history such as *A History of the Wife*, *Birth of the Chess Queen*, and *How the French Invented Love*, as well as her final book released posthumously, *Innocent Witnesses: Childhood Memories of World War II*. They were married for sixty-five years.

March 2021 | Hardcover | $24.00 | 9781503613768 | Redwood Press

CONVERSATION STARTERS

1. From the onset, we know that Marilyn is facing a terminal illness. She convinces her husband Irv to drop everything to write about their "final dance of life." How did their 65 years together make reading *A Matter of Death and Life* more relatable?

2. Did their professional experience—for instance, Marilyn's ability to describe the numbness of facing death and Irv's memories of past therapy sessions with bereaved patients—bring up specific ways for you to start talking about death and grieving in your own life?

3. Marilyn's Chapter 8 title, "Whose Death is this Anyway?", is a great example of how humor was so important to their facing life—and was always going to be part of how they faced death. Are there other places in the book where you found yourself laughing unexpectedly?

4. How have you used laughter to face hardships and grief in your own life?

5. In Chapter 9, Irv discusses the "rippling effect" described in Saint Paul's epistles, which came to mind as he grappled with the ripples Marilyn's life has left for her loved ones. Does looking at the ripples of life help in grief? Or make it harder to accept?

6. In Chapter 12, one of Marilyn's friends creates a one-edition book titled *Letters to Marilyn* in which her friends share their appreciation for her and help show the ripples of her life. When have you expressed or received the expression of ripples, and how might you show someone else their worth in a meaningful way?

7. The Yaloms share some practical and jarring information about facing death, such as in Chapter 16, where a doctor caring for Marilyn explains that she offers "physician-attended death" and not what is often termed "doctor-assisted suicide." Did their practical language mixed with intense love and commitment help make this idea easier to talk about?

8. Irv dedicated his life to helping the bereaved, and admits writing this book has changed him as a therapist. How has this book helped you with your own grief or in counseling others about grief?

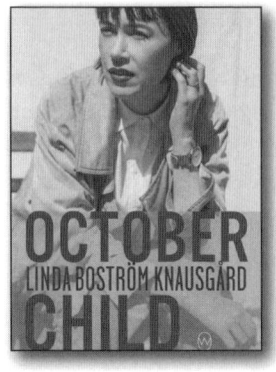

OCTOBER CHILD

Linda Boström Knausgård, translated by Saskia Vogel

From 2013 to 2017, Linda Boström Knausgård was periodically interned in a psychiatric ward where she was subjected to electroconvulsive therapy. As the treatments at this "factory" progressed, the writer's memories began to disappear. What good is a writer without her memory? This book, based on the author's experiences, is an eloquent and profound attempt to hold on to the past, to create a story, to make sense, and to keep alive ties to family, friends, and even oneself. Moments from childhood, youth, marriage, parenting, and divorce flicker across the pages of October Child. This is the story of one woman's struggle against mental illness and isolation. It is a raw testimony of how writing can preserve and heal.

"Swedish novelist Boström Knausgård brilliantly melds memoir and speculative nonfiction in her stirring account of the four years she spent in and out of a psychiatric ward ... Part fever-dream, part quest to retrieve her memories, Boström Knausgård's account expertly plumbs the treacherous crevasses of a creative mind." —**Publishers Weekly**

"(Boström Knausgård's) first openly autobiographical book becomes an act of self-examination powerful enough to match if not surpass those of her ex-husband's." —**The Guardian**

ABOUT THE AUTHOR: **Linda Boström Knausgård** is a Swedish author and poet, as well as a producer of documentaries for national radio. Her first novel, *The Helios Disaster*, was awarded the Mare Kandre Prize and shortlisted for the Swedish Radio Novel Award 2014. *Welcome to America*, her second novel, was nominated for the prestigious Swedish August Prize and the Svenska Dagbladet Literary Prize in her home country, and was also nominated for Best Translated Book Award in the United States. *October Child* became a bestseller in Sweden and throughout Scandinavia, where it was published to great critical acclaim.

June 2021 | Paperback | $16.99 | 9781642860894 | World Editions

CONVERSATION STARTERS

1. Are there any forms of agency available to our seemingly powerless narrator? If so, which ones?

2. In what ways are social classes discussed in the book? How does the narrator's perception of her social class contribute to her own identity?

3. Are the characters in the narrator's life supportive or dismissive of her adversity?

4. Who is Attila, encountered by the narrator towards the end of the book?

5. What is the narrator's relationship to physical places – houses, streets, wards, countries?

6. How does the protagonist bring her dreams and the events of her past life to the surface of this narrative? What effect does this have?

7. What does *October Child* say about the types of responsibilities we have towards others and ourselves? What happens when we fail in these responsibilities?

8. In what ways can writing – and reading – be cathartic?

9. If you have read Linda Boström Knausgård's other work, do you find any themes or characters that consistently reappear? Why do you believe they are important to her?

10. How does a real-life event transform when it becomes expressed in writing? Does writing things down fictionalize them, or preserve them, or both? What kind of transformation do you believe Linda Boström Knausgård sees in her writing?

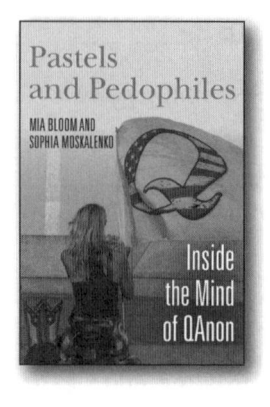

PASTELS AND PEDOPHILES: INSIDE THE MIND OF QANON
Mia Bloom & Sophia Moskalenko

In January 2021, thousands descended on the U.S. Capitol to aid President Trump in combating a shadowy cabal of Satan-worshipping pedophiles. Two women were among those who died that day. They, like millions of Americans, believed a mysterious insider known as "Q" is exposing a vast deep-state conspiracy. The QAnon conspiracy has ensnared many women, who identify as members of "pastel QAnon," answering the call to "save the children."

Pastels and Pedophiles explains why the rise of QAnon should not surprise us, tracking QAnon's unexpected leap from the darkest corners of the Internet to the filtered glow of yogi-mama Instagram, a frenzy fed by the COVID-19 pandemic that supercharged conspiracy theories and spurred a fresh wave of Q-inspired violence.

Pastels and Pedophiles connects the dots for readers, showing how a conspiracy theory with its roots in centuries-old anti-Semitic hate has adapted to encompass local grievances and has metastasized around the globe—appealing to a wide range of alienated people who feel something is not quite right in the world around them.

Finally, *Pastels and Pedophiles* lays out what can be done about QAnon's corrosive effect on society, to bring Q followers out of the rabbit hole and back into the light.

"A revealing—and disturbing—analysis of a dangerous threat to American democracy." —*Kirkus Review*

ABOUT THE AUTHORS: **Mia Bloom** is the International Security Fellow at New America, professor at Georgia State University, and member of the Evidence-Based Cybersecurity Research Group. She has authored books on violent extremism inclduing *Small Arms: Children and Terrorism*, *Bombshell: Women and Terrorism*, and *Dying to Kill: The Allure of Suicide Terror*.

Sophia Moskalenko is a psychologist studying mass identity, inter-group conflict, and conspiracy theories. She has written several books, including the award-winning *Friction: How Conflict Radicalizes Them and Us* and *The Marvel of Martyrdom: The Power of Self-Sacrifice in the Selfish World*.

June 2021 | Hardcover | $20.00 | 9781503630291 | Redwood Press

CONVERSATION STARTERS

1. What has facilitated the growth of QAnon believers since 2019? Why do you think 37% of Americans are unsure of whether the theory's allegations are completely false?

2. If, as the authors note in Chapter 1, "most followers of QAnon don't necessarily care who [Q] actually is," why does discovering Q's identity matter? Do you believe this revelation would help to unravel QAnon? How?

3. What is it that makes conspiracy believers persist in their beliefs, even when their evidence is openly disproved?

4. As Bloom and Moskalenko discuss the indoctrination of women into the QAnon conspiracy, several connections to cult and terrorist groups are insinuated. What distinguishes QAnon from these types of groups?

5. Why do we generally assume women are less violent or radical than men? How does this belief affect how we perceive and react to women in groups like that of QAnon?

6. In Chapter 2, we learn that factors like "widespread distrust of authority, anger at powerful figures in politics … and growing income inequality" can make people susceptible to conspiracy theories. How can we heal this anger and mistrust in our country, communities, and personal lives?

7. The state of 'unfreezing', in which unfortunate circumstances suddenly separate an individual from their communities and previous purpose, can happen to anyone, setting the unfrozen individual on a quest to find a new direction and community. How have you reacted to moments of 'unfreezing' in your life?

8. Bloom and Moskalenko note that shifting ideas of gender and its correlated roles have "cracked" the worldview of many Americans, particularly that of women. What can we do to help people adjust to these types of changes more smoothly?

9. There's a line in Chapter 3 which states: "The cost of building online connections is alienation from real-life ones." Do you believe this is true? How has your time on social media affected your relationships with others? Do you believe it is possible to create 'real-life' relationships via social media? Why?

10. How can the attitude inoculation approach suggested in Chapter 4 be applied to your own life?

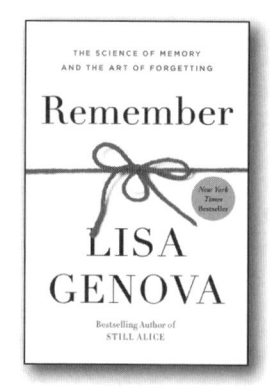

REMEMBER: THE SCIENCE OF MEMORY AND THE ART OF FORGETTING
Lisa Genova

A fascinating exploration of the intricacies of how we remember, why we forget, and what we can do to protect our memories, from the Harvard-trained neuroscientist and bestselling author of *Still Alice*.

In *Remember*, neuroscientist and acclaimed novelist Lisa Genova delves into how memories are made and how we retrieve them. You'll learn whether forgotten memories are temporarily inaccessible or erased forever and why some memories are built to exist for only a few seconds (like a passcode) while others can last a lifetime (your wedding day). You'll come to appreciate the clear distinction between normal forgetting (where you parked your car) and forgetting due to Alzheimer's (that you own a car). And you'll see how memory is profoundly impacted by meaning, emotion, sleep, stress, and context. Once you understand the language of memory and how it functions, its incredible strengths and maddening weaknesses, its natural vulnerabilities and potential superpowers, you can both vastly improve your ability to remember and feel less rattled when you inevitably forget. You can set educated expectations for your memory, and in doing so, create a better relationship with it. You don't have to fear it anymore. And that can be life-changing.

"Using her expertise as a neuroscientist and her gifts as a storyteller, Lisa Genova explains the nuances of human memory." —**Steve Pinker**

ABOUT THE AUTHOR: **Lisa Genova** is the *New York Times* bestselling author of the novels *Still Alice*, *Left Neglected*, *Love Anthony*, *Inside the O'Briens*, and *Every Note Played*. *Still Alice* was adapted into an Oscar-winning film starring Julianne Moore. Lisa travels worldwide speaking about memory and brain health and has appeared on The Dr. Oz Show, Today, PBS NewsHour, CNN, and was featured in the PBS Special, Building a Better Memory Through Science. Her TED talks, What You Can Do to Prevent Alzheimer's and How Your Memory Works have been viewed over 7 million times.

March 2021 | Hardcover | $26.99 | 9780593137956 | Harmony Books

CONVERSATION STARTERS

1. Did you imagine the penny at beginning of the book? Did you envision it with 100% accuracy? If not, why did you misremember what a penny looks like even though you've seen one hundreds of times?

2. The author suggests that because we remember what we pay attention to, we might want to be mindful about what we focus on. What do you pay attention to? Might that change now, having read the book?

3. What are some things you remember from ten, twenty, thirty years ago? Having read Remember, why do you think you've retained these experiences and information and not others?

4. List some things you can do based on "muscle memory." What did it take to create those memories/abilities?

5. Flashbulb memories are memories for experiences that carried big emotion, were highly unexpected, felt personal, and can be vividly recalled years later. Do you have any flashbulb memories?

6. Memories for what happened can change over time and with each recall. Might some of your memories have drifted from how events actually played out?

7. Why do we experience more "tip of the tongue" moments with proper names, titles, and places versus regular nouns?

8. Prospective memory is your memory for what you intend to do later, and all human brains are poorly designed for this kind of recall. What kinds of external aids can you use to augment your prospective memory (dis)ability?

9. We tend to villainize forgetting. Has your perspective on forgetting changed? In what instances might forgetting be beneficial? Where can you relax?

10. How much sleep do you get? Knowing how essential a good night's sleep is for memory, are you reconsidering your nighttime routine or changing your sleep habits?

11. What's your biggest takeaway from the book?

12. Has your relationship with your memory changed? How so?

THIS TIME NEXT YEAR WE'LL BE LAUGHING: A MEMOIR
Jacqueline Winspear

A 2021 Edgar Award Nominee for Best Critical/Biographical

The *New York Times* bestselling author of the Maisie Dobbs series offers a deeply personal memoir of her family's resilience in the face of war and privation.

After sixteen novels, Jacqueline Winspear has taken the bold step of turning to memoir, revealing the hardships and joys of her family history. Both shockingly frank and deftly restrained, her story tackles the difficult, poignant, and fascinating family accounts of her paternal grandfather's shellshock; her mother's evacuation from London during the Blitz; her soft-spoken animal-loving father's torturous assignment to an explosives team during WWII; her parents' years living with Romany Gypsies; and Winspear's own childhood picking hops and fruit on farms in rural Kent, capturing her ties to the land and her dream of being a writer at its very inception.

An eye-opening and heartfelt portrayal of a post-War England we rarely see, *This Time Next Year We'll Be Laughing* chronicles a childhood in the English countryside, of working class indomitability and family secrets, of artistic inspiration and the price of memory.

"Jacqueline Winspear has created a memoir of her English childhood that is every bit as engaging as her Maisie Dobbs novels, just as rich in character and detail, history and humanity. Her writing is lovely, elegant and welcoming."
—**Anne Lamott**

ABOUT THE AUTHOR: **Jacqueline Winspear** was born and raised in Kent, England. After graduating from the University of London's Institute of Education, she worked in academic publishing, higher education, and marketing communications. She emigrated to the United States in 1990. She has written fifteen novels in the *New York Times* bestselling Maisie Dobbs series, which has won numerous awards, including the Agatha, Macavity, and Alex. Her standalone novel about the Great War, *The Care and Management of Lies*, was a finalist for the Dayton Literary Peace Prize. She lives in California.

November 2020 | Hardcover | $27.95 | 9781641292696 | Soho Press
September 2021 | Paperback | 16.95 | 9781641292696 | Soho Press

CONVERSATION STARTERS

1. In your opinion, how much of this memoir is Winspear's own story, and how much is it her parents'? Is she offering anecdotes from her parents' lives in order to contextualize her own life story, or because they have become her own life story—or both?

2. On memoir, Winspear says, "we don't just look back at an event in our past; we are remembering the memory of what happened." What do you think she means by that? Is that how you would describe memoir? How are memory, memoir, and history similar or different?

3. In several episodes from her childhood, Winspear describes being profoundly affected by things she learned about women who lived in her neighborhood; in several cases, she recollects that their stories pointed her toward novels she would later write. Do you have personal memories like this from your childhood—people who you might not have known well, but whom you still think about decades later because of something they said or did, or who affected the way you think or live your life?

4. The title of the book comes from Winspear's father's oft-repeated saying during hard times, "this time next year we'll be laughing." Do you relate to that phrase? Were there particular examples of perseverance during hard times in the book resonated with you? Do you or does someone in your family have a maxim that you look to for reassurance?

5. The theme of war-era PTSD runs through the personal stories of both sides of Jacqueline Winspear's family, and she discusses the scientifically proven theory that traumas can be hereditary. Is her family story a very British one? Or are there comparable or analogous American stories about the "Greatest Generation" or the generation born between the two World Wars?

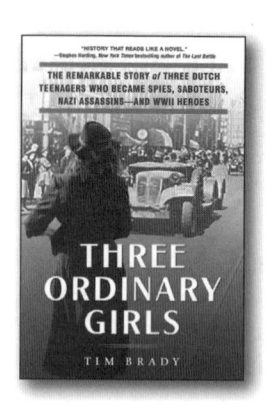

THREE ORDINARY GIRLS: THE REMARKABLE STORY OF THREE DUTCH TEENAGERS WHO BECAME SPIES, SABOTEURS, NAZI ASSASSINS— AND WWII HEROES
Tim Brady

The astonishing true story of three fearless female resisters during WWII whose youth and innocence belied their extraordinary daring in the Nazi-occupied Netherlands.

Truus Oversteegen, her younger sister Freddie, and their friend Hannie Schaft, were just teenagers when the commander of The Dutch Royal Army surrendered to the Nazis. Overnight, nine million Netherlanders were suddenly under the heel of the Nazi boot. The German-controlled government quickly began to restrict the lives of Dutch Jews and then to ship them off to camps in Germany and Eastern Europe. The girls soon felt compelled to resist.

As Anne Frank and her family were just going into hiding only miles away in Amsterdam, the girls started with simple acts of covert illegality: lifting German ID cards to counterfeit them; distributing fliers announcing strikes, passing out anti-Nazi literature. With each initiative, the danger became more pronounced, the stakes higher.

Soon they were called on for bigger, deadlier jobs: Ferrying Jewish children to safeguard locations. Stockpiling weapons. Detonating bombs. Intelligence-gathering. Spying. Sabotage. Murder. With each assignment, they became an integral part of the Dutch resistance. But it was not without peril, heartache, suffering, or loss. Award-winning historian Tim Brady paints a vivid portrait of Tuus, Freddie, and Hannie, three ordinary Dutch girls whose selfless acts of courage as they sought to undermine the Nazis and their Dutch collaborators were nothing short of extraordinary.

"Brady conveys the inhumanity of the period with precision ... This moving story spotlights the extraordinary heroism of everyday people during the war and the Holocaust." —**Publishers Weekly**

ABOUT THE AUTHOR: **Tim Brady** is an award-winning writer of numerous historical nonfiction books and television documentaries. He lives in St. Paul, Minnesota, and is a graduate of the Iowa Writers' Workshop.

February 2021 | Hardcover | $26.00 | 9780806540382 | Citadel Press
April 2022 | Paperback | $15.95 | 9780806540399 | Citadel Press

CONVERSATION STARTERS

1. Many women served in the underground resistance during WWII. What makes the stories of Truus, Freddie, and Hannie so remarkable?

2. Hannie Schaft's background was very different from that of Truus and Freddie Oversteegen, but the three joined forces despite their differences. What were the events that drew them together?

3. Truus, Freddie, and Hannie came of age during a tumultuous moment in 1930s Europe. How did life in their medieval village of Haarlem change after the commander of The Dutch Royal Army surrendered to the Nazis and nine million Netherlanders were suddenly under the heel of the German boot?

4. Hannie, Truus, and Freddie had a strong sense of social justice at a young age. How did that come about?

5. Do you think you would have aided in the Resistance if you had lived in the Netherlands during WWII? Why or why not?

6. How did the Hannie and the Oversteegen sisters use misconceptions about youth and teenage girls to their advantage?

7. The girls had mixed feelings about what they did in the name of the Resistance, but not in the Resistance itself. How did that conflict make you think about what constitutes duty and bravery?

8. The girls started with simple acts of covert illegality: lifting German ID cards to counterfeit them; distributing fliers announcing strikes, passing out anti-Nazi literature. But with each mission, the stakes got higher and their acts became more dangerous, evolving into stockpiling weapons, detonating bombs, spying, sabotage, and murder. Do you think they ever went too far?

9. Is there anything you would be willing to risk your life for the way Hannie, Freddie, and Truus did?

10. The stories of Hannie Schaft and the Oversteegen sisters are quite well-known in the Netherlands, but few people in the United States are aware of them. Why do you think that is?

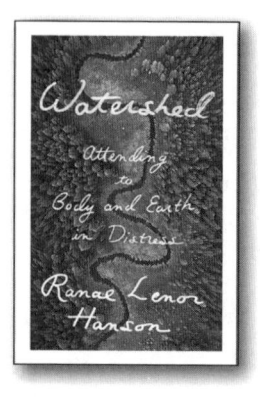

WATERSHED: ATTENDING TO BODY AND EARTH IN DISTRESS
Ranae Lenor Hanson

The body of the earth, beset by a climate in crisis, experiences drought much like the human body experiences thirst, as Ranae Lenor Hanson's body did as a warning sign of the disease that would change her life: Type 1 diabetes. What if we tended to an ailing ecosystem just as Hanson learned to care for herself in the throes of a chronic medical condition. This is the possibility explored in a work that is at once a memoir of illness and health, a contemplation of the surrounding natural world in distress, and a reflection on the ways these come together in personal, local, and global opportunities for healing. When, in the grip of a global pandemic, humans drastically change their behavior to preserve human life, we also see how the earth breathes more freely as a result. In light of that lesson, *Watershed* helps us to consider our place and our part in the health and healing of the world around us.

"The credo 'water is life' has become a key environmental rallying cry in the years since Standing Rock, and this book helps us remember why. It recalls an American past, inhabits a global present, and imagines a working future—it will be an aid to many as they grapple with our difficult moment."
—**Bill McKibben, founder of 350.org and author of** *The End of Nature*

"In a direct and often wise voice, through a series of moving, revealing, and entertaining stories, Watershed *makes clear the connection between climate change and our own bodies."* —**Susan Griffin, author of** *Woman and Nature*

*"*Watershed *shows us that the harm we have wrought on the world is no longer a future problem to be solved."* —**Eric Utne, founder,** *Utne Reader*

ABOUT THE AUTHOR: An educator and committed climate activist, **Ranae Lenor Hanson** taught writing and global studies at Minneapolis College for thirty-one years.

May 2021 | Paperback | $19.95 | 9781517910976 | University of Minnesota Press

CONVERSATION STARTERS

1. Similarities between diabetes and climate disruption form central images in the book. Which of the comparisons raised resonated for you? Do you have other health conditions that you find mirrored in ecological stress and well-being?

2. At the beginning of the book, the author acknowledges the Indigenous Peoples of the lands she has lived on. At the end, she offers ethical principles as Winona LaDuke spoke them. How does the relationship between the author and Ojibwe people develop? Is that presentation respectful? What attitude does the author suggest readers should take toward the Original Peoples of their own lands? What connection do you have to the people who are indigenous to your home?

3. The sections between chapters offer suggestions for contemplation and action. Which of those meditations or actions did you follow? What did you experience as you did that? Which of those might you suggest to others? What suggestions would you develop yourself?

4. The book relies on personal stories from varied people to give evidence of both harm to and the resilience of ecological communities and the individual bodies that make up those communities. Which stories reached you? Eyewitness reports are not conclusive evidence, so the book also includes statistics. How well did you feel the stories and the statistics supported each other? What further evidence might you seek out to support or refute the claims made in the book?

5. How does the book reveal racial and economic injustice, especially related to diabetes and climate trauma? How did you respond to the stories and the troubles presented? What have you experienced of this yourself? What actions might you be called to that could further justice, health, and all-life connection?

6. *Watershed* focuses on Minnesota communities and waters. To what extent do you find it to speak for waters and their interdependent beings in other areas of earth? What messages could you carry to your home?

YOUNG ADULT

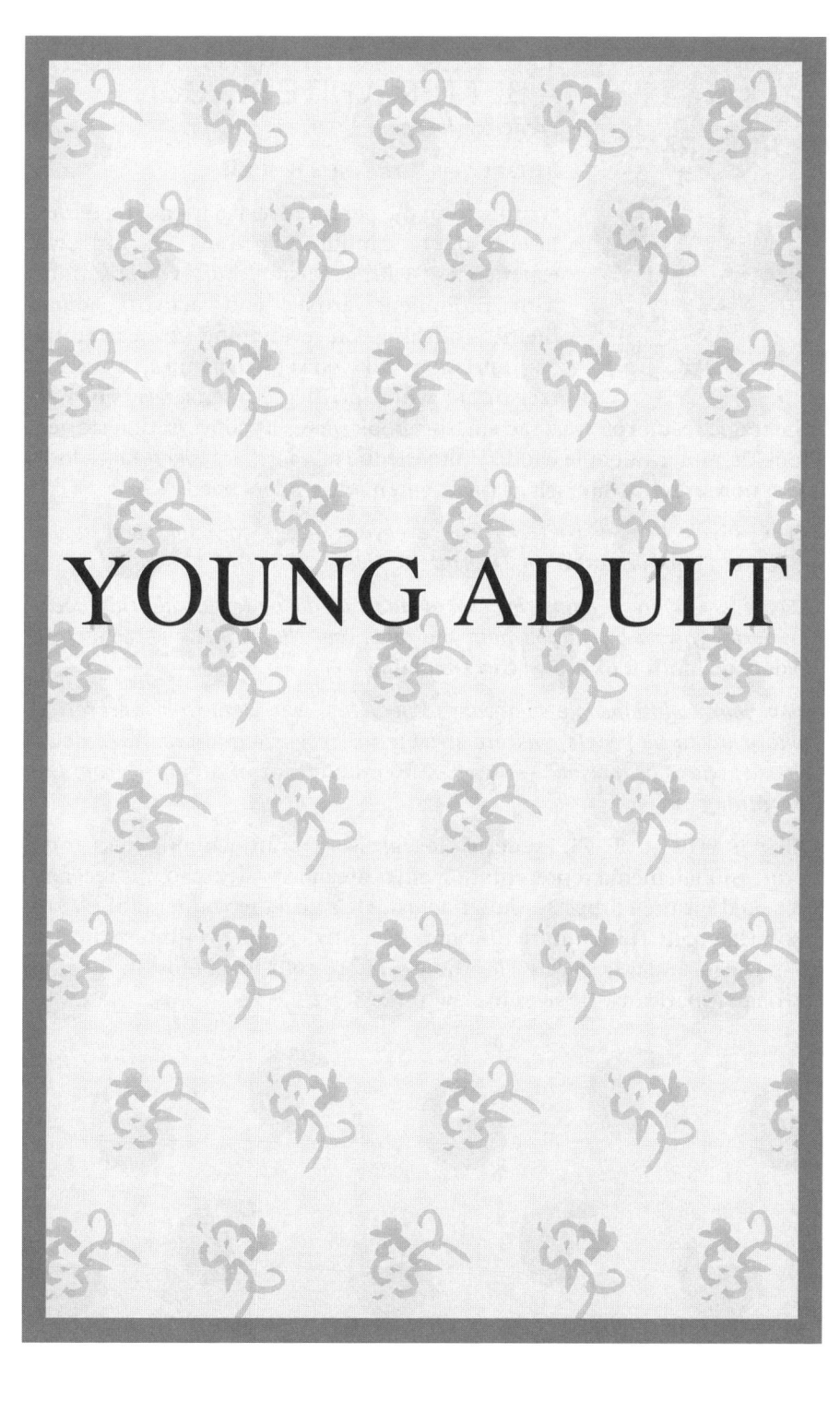

THE BLACK FRIEND: ON BEING A BETTER WHITE PERSON

Frederick Joseph

Instant *New York Times* **Bestseller**

Writing from the perspective of a friend, Frederick Joseph offers candid reflections on his own experiences with racism and conversations with prominent artists and activists about theirs. Touching on everything from cultural appropriation to power dynamics, "reverse racism" to white privilege, microaggressions to the tragic results of overt racism, this book serves as conversation starter, tool kit, and invaluable window into the life of a former "token Black kid" who now presents himself as the friend many readers need.

"*The Black Friend is* THE *book everyone needs to read right now.*" —**Angie Thomas, author of** *The Hate U Give*

"*For every white person who ever wanted to do better, inside this book, Frederick Joseph offers you both the tools and the chance.*" —**Jacqueline Woodson, author of** *Brown Girl Dreaming*

"*For young white people who want to be better, who want to be anti-racist, who want to be people who are striving to recognize and even take down the structures of racism.*" —**Ibram X. Kendi, author of** *Stamped from the Beginning*

ABOUT THE AUTHOR: **Frederick Joseph** is an award-winning marketing professional, media representation advocate, and writer who was recently selected for the Forbes 30 Under 30 list. He's also the winner of the 2018 Bob Clampett Humanitarian Award, given by Comic-Con International: San Diego, and was selected for the 2018 Root 100 List of Most Influential African Americans. He lives in New York City.

December 2021 | Hardcover | $17.99 | 9781536217018 | Candlewick Press

CONVERSATION STARTERS

1. Who benefits and how from distorted narratives taught about topics such as the first Thanksgiving and Christopher Columbus as well as the silencing and erasure of BIPOC? How does this play a role in conditioning and socializing young people into racism?

2. In what ways have you noticed a color-blind approach taken toward race? Who benefits from color blindness and in what ways? How are BIPOC harmed when white people suggest it's better to be color-blind?

3. How do movements that leverage social media to promote activism, such as #OscarsSoWhite, #RepresentationMatters, #BlackLivesMatter, and #weneeddiversebooks work to disrupt racism and bring awareness to the importance of inclusivity?

4. What distinctions can you make between cultural exchange, cultural appreciation, and cultural appropriation? What does it mean for white people to engage with stories that are not their own and to understand that they are not for them?

5. Joseph writes, "Some people think they can be an ally while also letting the people close to them continue to be comfortable in their racism" (120). Do you think it's truly possible to be an anti-racist and associate with racist people? Why or why not?

6. There has been a legacy of whiteness being used as a weapon against Black people in the United States. Amy Cooper's false accusation of Black birdwatcher Christian Cooper is one example of this. In what ways have Black people had to navigate and work to safeguard themselves from white privilege and the power white people hold within the justice system?

7. When BIPOC speak about racism they've experienced, there can be a tendency for some white listeners to become defensive and conflate their own experiences. "All Lives Matter" is one example of this that Joseph shares. Consider why this is offensive. What does it mean to truly listen and learn during discussions about race and racism?

8. How do you define and differentiate between ally and accomplice? Where might you locate yourself on this continuum? Why is allyship insufficient in the work of anti-racism?

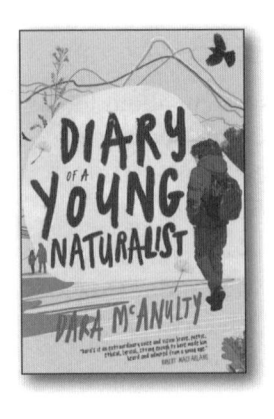

DIARY OF A YOUNG NATURALIST
Dara McAnulty

From sixteen-year-old Dara McAnulty, a globally renowned figure in the youth climate activist movement, comes a memoir about loving the natural world and fighting to save it.

Diary of a Young Naturalist chronicles the turning of a year in Dara's Northern Ireland home patch. Beginning in spring—when "the sparrows dig the moss from the guttering and the air is as puffed out as the robin's chest"—these diary entries about his connection to wildlife and the way he sees the world are vivid, evocative, and moving.

As well as Dara's intense connection to the natural world, *Diary of a Young Naturalist* captures his perspective as a teenager juggling exams, friendships, and a life of campaigning. We see his close-knit family, the disruptions of moving and changing schools, and the complexities of living with autism. "In writing this book," writes Dara, "I have experienced challenges but also felt incredible joy, wonder, curiosity and excitement. In sharing this journey my hope is that people of all generations will not only understand autism a little more but also appreciate a child's eye view on our delicate and changing biosphere."

Winner of the Wainwright Prize for UK nature writing and already sold into more than a dozen territories, *Diary of a Young Naturalist* is a triumphant debut from an important new voice.

"Dara's is an extraordinary voice and vision: brave, poetic, ethical, lyrical, strong enough to have made him heard and admired from a young age."
—**Robert Macfarlane**

ABOUT THE AUTHOR: **Dara McAnulty** is the author of *Diary of a Young Naturalist* and the recipient of the Wainwright Prize for nature writing. Dara lives with his mum, dad, brother Lorcan, sister Bláthnaid and rescue greyhound Rosie in County Down, Northern Ireland. Dara's love for nature, his activism and his honesty about autism, has earned him a huge social media following from across the world and many accolades: in 2017 he was awarded BBC Springwatch 'Unsprung Hero' Award; in 2018 he became ambassador for RSPCA and the iWill campaign; in 2019 he became a Young Ambassador for the Jane Goodall Institute and became the youngest ever recipient of the RSPB Medal for conservation.

June 2021 | Hardcover | $25.00 | 9781571311801 | Milkweed Editions

CONVERSATION STARTERS

1. How does the separation of chapters by season draw parallels between Dara McAnulty's experience and transformation as a person and naturalist?

2. McAnulty often compares nature and its transformation to magic. Give three examples of how he makes these connections.

3. In *Diary of a Young Naturalist*, McAnulty references the idea of isolation and separating oneself from the general public: "Over the years, a wall of stone and beautiful ivy has grown around me, and only family and wildlife are allowed in" (137). On page 208, McAnulty writes, "I'm so used to keeping my thoughts locked inside and being in a space where it's only me and my family." How do these comparisons relate to Dara's identity as a naturalist? As a neurodivergent individual?

4. On page 15, in reference to the living and breathing flora and fauna in the natural world McAnulty writes, "They all make sense to me, people just don't." Where else has McAnulty reflected on these feelings, and how has it deepened his relationship with the natural world?

5. How does McAnulty discuss a human's strong relationship with nature in relation to the idea of balance and symmetry?

6. On page 64, McAnulty writes, "Autism makes me feel everything more intensely: I don't have a joy filter." How might his identity and experience relate to his relationship with the natural world?

7. McAnulty mentions several fauna and flora in *Diary of a Young Naturalist*, but he returns to birds several times throughout the book. How does McAnulty describe the significance of birds in his world and the natural world?

8. How does McAnulty describe his relationship with his family and its importance to his foundation?

9. On page 158, McAnulty refers to his visit and speech at Dublin's Dead Zoo, and how speaking out empowered him ("I might love punk music and hate conformity and being boxed in, but I never saw myself as a rebel. But maybe I am, and as I stand on a wooden box, the organiser, called Caroline, holds a microphone so I can read my speech. I feel emboldened, outspoken. I feel like it's the first time I've actually said out loud all the many things I'm angry about"). How can readers of *Diary of a Young Naturalist* be more engaged environmental activists in their own communities?

INDIVISIBLE
Daniel Aleman

This timely, moving debut novel follows a teen's efforts to keep his family together as his parents face deportation.

Mateo Garcia and his younger sister, Sophie, have been taught to fear one word for as long as they can remember: deportation. Over the past few years, however, the fear that their undocumented immigrant parents could be sent back to Mexico has started to fade. Ma and Pa have been in the United States for so long, they have American-born children, and they're hard workers and good neighbors. When Mateo returns from school one day to find that his parents have been taken by ICE, he realizes that his family's worst nightmare has become a reality. With his parents' fate and his own future hanging in the balance, Mateo must figure out who he is and what he is capable of, even as he's forced to question what it means to be an American.

Daniel Aleman's *Indivisible* is a remarkable story—both powerful in its explorations of immigration in America and deeply intimate in its portrait of a teen boy driven by his fierce, protective love for his parents and his sister.

"Deeply moving. A potent reminder that no human being is illegal." —**Jodi Picoult**, *New York Times* **bestselling author of** *The Book of Two Ways*

"A powerful story about family, friendship, and home." —**Yamile Saied Méndez, author of Pura Belpré Inaugural YA Award winner** *Furia*

"A gripping harrowing story about an American tragedy." —**Kelly Loy Gilbert, author of Stonewall Honor Book** *Picture Us In the Light*

ABOUT THE AUTHOR: **Daniel Aleman** was born and raised in Mexico City. A graduate of McGill University, he is passionate about books, coffee, and Mexican food. After spending time in Montreal and the New York City area, he now lives in Toronto, where is on a never-ending search for the best tacos in the city. You can connect with him on Twitter (@Dan_Aleman), Instagram (@danaleman) or at danielaleman.com

May 2021 | Hardcover | $18.99 | 9780759556058 |
Little, Brown Books for Young Readers
August 2022 | Paperback | $10.99 | 9780759553897 |
Little, Brown Books for Young Readers

CONVERSATION STARTERS

1. Mateo's Ma says that he "feels too much." How does this both work for and against Mateo? When do Mateo's feelings, negative or positive, most color his experience?

2. Mateo and his friends all present different versions of themselves to the world. How do they adapt their personalities to fit their surroundings? Why do you think people change their behavior based on their setting?

3. Throughout the book, Mateo wrestles with the cost of the opportunities provided by his parents' sacrifices. How does his perspective compare with that of his parents? How does the pressure to succeed impact Mateo's dreams for his life?

4. Mateo's Ma reminds him of the "'be careful' rule": "Don't say anything. No one can know." How does keeping secrets affect Mateo? What additional stressors does this rule add to his daily life?

5. Mrs. Solis tells Mateo that "sometimes, the only way to be strong is to let someone else carry some of the weight with you." How does asking for help make you stronger? How do communities support their own? When Mateo opens himself up to support from those around him, how does he change?

6. Amy reassures Sophie after a schoolmate makes a xenophobic statement about Sophie's parents. What does it mean to be an ally? How do characters provide allyship to Mateo and Sophie?

7. Multiple characters benefit from intergenerational relationships. How does the lived reality of one generation impact subsequent generations?

8. Each member of Mateo's family experiences Pa and Ma's deportation in different ways. How are their experiences similar? What differences do you see in their experiences?

9. Kimmie and Mateo discuss the expectations other people have of their identities. How do race and sexuality affect the societal expectations placed on young people?

10. Mateo affirms that "no matter how hard they tried to separate us, how much the distance hurt, or how it nearly broke us, we are really, truly indivisible." While physically separated, how do Mateo, Sophie, and their parents try to maintain closeness to one another? What emotional walls complicate those efforts?

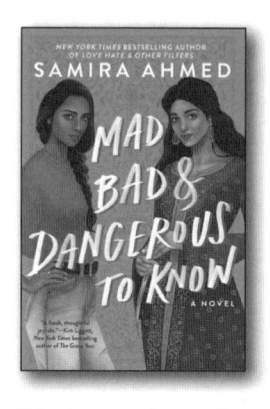

MAD, BAD & DANGEROUS TO KNOW
Samira Ahmed

Smash the patriarchy. Eat all the pastries.

Discover *New York Times* bestseller Samira Ahmed's romantic, sweeping adventure through the streets of Paris told in alternating narratives that bridge centuries, continents, and the lives of two young Muslim women fighting to write their own stories.

It's August in Paris and 17-year-old Khayyam Maquet—American, French, Indian, Muslim—is at a crossroads. This holiday with her parents should be a dream trip for the budding art historian. But her maybe-ex-boyfriend is ghosting her, she might have just blown her chance at getting into her dream college, and now all she really wants is to be back home in Chicago figuring out her messy life instead of brooding in the City of Light.

Two hundred years before Khayyam's summer of discontent, Leila is struggling to survive and keep her true love hidden from the Pasha who has "gifted" her with favored status in his harem. In the present day—and with the company of Alex, a très charmant teen descendant of Alexandre Dumas—Khayyam searches for a rumored lost painting, uncovering a connection between Leila and Alexandre Dumas, Eugène Delacroix, and Lord Byron that may have been erased from history.

"Lively and passionate, this book tackles issues of cultural identity and examines which stories are passed down through time – all while indulging in a romantic amateur sleuthing romp through the City of Lights." —**NPR.org**

"A fierce, feminist coming-of-age story." —*Bustle*

ABOUT THE AUTHOR: **Samira Ahmed** was born in Bombay, India, and grew up in a small town in Illinois in a house that smelled like fried onions, cardamom, and potpourri. A graduate of the University of Chicago, she's lived in Vermont, Chicago, New York City, and Kauai, where she spent a year searching for the perfect mango. Follow her on Twitter and Instagram @sam_aye_ahm.

April 2020 | Hardcover | $18.99 | 9781616959890 | Soho Teen
July 2021 | Paperback | $10.99 | 9781641292313 | Soho Teen

CONVERSATION STARTERS

1. Khayyam's very first words to the reader are, "I live between spaces." Why does she feel that way? How do those words foreshadow one of the novel's themes?

2. Why does Leila hate the title of "haseki" when it means "the favored?" And how does her first chapter foreshadow her destiny—both while she was alive and after her death?

3. Look at Delacroix's paintings The Combat of the Giaour and The Combat of the Giaour and Hassan. What story do the images in the painting tell? What part of the story do they leave out?

4. Khayyam, Leila, Alexandre, Zaid, Byron, and Dumas all conceal things or tell lies. What are the different costs they pay for their lies? Are some lies justified? Do some lies "weigh" more than others?

5. Why is Khayyam hesitant about sharing Leila's story with the world when she and Alexandre finally start discovering the real truth? Why does she change her mind? Was that the right choice?

6. Who decides what history is written and what stories are pushed aside? How does racism and patriarchy play a role in that? How would you decide what stories and accomplishments deserve to be known and remembered?

7. Why does Leila tell Byron, "I have much more to fear from men than jinn?" Does that ring true in her life?

8. Different men tried to use Khayyam and Leila as means to their desired ends. How do Khayyam and Leila fight that?

9. Khayyam and Leila lived in very different times but both struggle to find their voice and tell their own stories. What similar forces were they fighting against? What societal change allowed Khayyam to have more freedoms than Leila? How did she choose to use that power and privilege? Why does Leila choose to finally write her own story?

10. What is eternal return? How does it play out in the novel? Is it real?

MAYBE WE'RE ELECTRIC
Val Emmich

Tegan Everly is quiet. Known around school simply as the girl with the hand, she's usually only her most outspoken self with her friend Neel, and right now they're not exactly talking. When Tegan is ambushed by her mom with a truth she can't face, she flees home in a snowstorm, finding refuge at a forgotten local attraction—the tiny Thomas Edison museum.

She's not alone for long. In walks Mac Durant. Striking, magnetic, a gifted athlete, Mac Durant is the classmate adored by all. Tegan can't stand him. Even his name sounds fake. Except the Mac Durant she thinks she knows isn't the one before her now—this Mac is rattled and asking her for help.

Over one unforgettable night spent consuming antique records and corner-shop provisions, Tegan and Mac cast aside their public personas and family pressures long enough to forge an unexpectedly charged bond and—in the very spot in New Jersey that inspired Edison's boldest creations—totally reinvent themselves. But could Tegan's most shameful secret destroy what they've built?

Emotionally vivid and endlessly charming, *Maybe We're Electric* is an artfully woven meditation on how pain can connect us—we can carry it alone in darkness or share the burden and watch the world light up again.

"A poignant, gemlike novel about grief, regret, and loneliness." —**Kathleen Glasgow,** *New York Times*-**bestselling author of** *Girl in Pieces*

"Written with tenderness and heart, this is a book that will light readers up." —**Abdi Nazemian, author of Stonewall Honor Book** *Like a Love Story*

ABOUT THE AUTHOR: **Val Emmich** is a *New York Times* bestselling author, singer-songwriter, and actor. His novels include *The Reminders* and *Dear Evan Hansen: The Novel*, the adaptation of the hit Broadway show.

September 2021 | Hardcover | $17.99 | 9780316535700 |
Poppy/Little, Brown Books for Young Readers

CONVERSATION STARTERS

1. Why is Tegan quiet? Why is Mac not?

2. Tegan hates being "the girl with the hand." Why doesn't she want to put her limb difference on display like others choose to do on social media?

3. Why does Tegan find it easier to speak up on social media? Why does she try on different social media personas? Why do you think she becomes Nightshade?

4. Why does Tegan struggle to give up Nightshade? How does she feel guilty for what she did and also proud of what she achieved?

5. How does Mac's family's dynamic change when his brother, James, leaves for college?

6. Why does Mac ask Tegan to make the 911 call at the start of the novel?

7. Tegan's dad gives her the advice of finding space wherever you can. What do you think he means?

8. How can you relate to Mac saying, "It's like I remember the things I want to forget and forget the things I wish I could remember" (118)?

9. Why do you think people like a simple story (162)?

10. Neel says, "There's a difference between joking around and just being plain mean" (177). How can people mask unkindness as a joke?

11. Is Neel a good friend to Tegan? Is Tegan a good friend to Neel?

12. Tegan admits to herself that sometimes she ignores Neel's advice "not because I don't agree with it, but because I'm not strong enough to do what's right" (181). What gives her the courage to do what is right?

13. How is Tegan's relationship with her mom complicated? What about her relationship with Charlie? What shifts for her with both?

14. At the end of the novel, Tegan thinks, "I'm scared, but I'm not alone" (273). How is Mac also scared but not alone? How about you?

15. How is Thomas Edison the third main character in the story? What do he and the museum symbolize?

16. Would you have forgiven Tegan?

17. Why does being seen matter so much?

THE NATURE OF WITCHES
Rachel Griffin

From a stunning new voice in fantasy comes the fierce, romantic story about a world on the brink of destruction, the one witch who holds the power to save it, and the choice that could cost her everything she loves.

For centuries, witches have maintained the climate, but now their control is faltering as the atmosphere becomes more erratic; the storms, more destructive. All hope lies with Clara, a once-in-a-generation Everwitch whose magic is tied to every season.

In Autumn, Clara wants nothing to do with her power. It's wild and volatile, and the price of her magic—losing the ones she loves—is too high, despite the need to control the increasingly dangerous weather.

In Winter, the world is on the precipice of disaster. Fires burn, storms rage, and Clara accepts that she's the only one who can make a difference.

In Spring, she falls for Sang, the witch training her. As her magic grows, so do her feelings, until she's terrified Sang will be the next one she loses.

In Summer, Clara must choose between her power and her happiness, her duty and the people she loves ... before she loses Sang, her magic, and thrusts the world into chaos

"A bright, fresh read from a glowing new voice." —**Adrienne Young,** *New York Times* **bestselling author of** *Fable*

"[A] masterfully told story. I couldn't love this book more." —**Shea Ernshaw,** *New York Times* **bestselling author of** *The Wicked Deep* **and** *Winterwood*

"A magnificent debut ... I'm obsessed." —**Adalyn Grace,** *New York Times* **bestselling author of** *All the Stars and Teeth*

ABOUT THE AUTHOR: **Rachel Griffin** lives just outside of Seattle with her husband and dog, Doppler. She was fortunate enough to witness the 2017 total solar eclipse and became a certified weather spotter for the National Weather Service while doing research for this project. *The Nature of Witches* is her debut.

June 2021 | Hardcover | $17.99 | 9781728229423 | Sourcebooks Fire

CONVERSATION STARTERS

1. What season witch would you be and why?

2. Clara's school isolated her to protect the other students, but there was very little attention paid to the effect separating her would have on Clara's well-being. How much did her isolation affect her decisions? Was the school wrong to separate her from her peers?

3. Mr. Burrows creates extreme tests for Clara that are risky and dangerous, but they also force Clara to access more magic than she ever has, making her stronger. Are his methods justified? Why or why not?

4. Mr. Hart had great affection for Clara. Mr. Burrows was callous, and yet he was able to push Clara's abilities to new heights. Were your most effective teachers the ones who treated you most kindly or the ones who pushed you the hardest? Are the two mutually exclusive?

5. When we first meet Clara, she hates that she changes with the seasons and craves consistency. Part of her journey is embracing change and learning to see it as a beautiful thing. In what ways has change played a powerful role in your life?

6. One of Clara's deepest fears is that she's too much for other people: too emotional, too inconsistent, too sensitive, too in her head. When she reads Mr. Hart's logbook and learns that he believed her magic flowed on a current of feeling, it enables her to change her perception of herself. Why do you think Mr. Hart believed Clara's depth of feeling is the source of her power?

7. Do you think Clara and Paige could have been happy together if Clara had learned to control her magic sooner?

8. Why do you think Sang is able to see Clara so clearly?

9. Climate change and environmentalism are major themes in the book. While it acknowledges the hard work the lies ahead, The Nature of Witches ultimately ends on a hopeful note. Do you feel hopeful about the future of our planet? Why or why not?

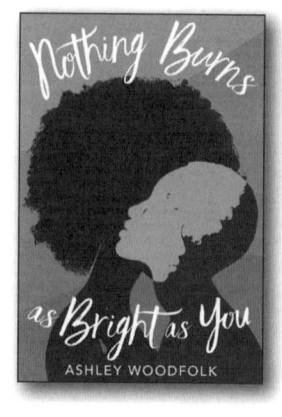

NOTHING BURNS AS BRIGHT AS YOU
Ashley Woodfolk

This emotionally charged novel in verse follows an intense and tumultuous relationship between two queer teen girls, anchored around a single day where they set a fire and their relationship spirals out of control. An unforgettable love story, *Nothing Burns As Bright As You* is a beautifully written, propulsive read that will take your breath away.

"A fierce, wrenching, deeply honest look at first love—I invite Ashley Woodfolk to break my heart with a book like this anytime." —**Leah Johnson, author of** *You Should See Me in a Crown*

ABOUT THE AUTHOR: **Ashley Woodfolk** has loved reading and writing for as long as she can remember. She graduated from Rutgers University and worked in children's book publishing for over a decade. Now a full-time mom and writer, Ashley lives in a sunny Brooklyn apartment with her cute husband, her cuter dog, and the cutest baby in the world. Her books include *The Beauty That Remains*, *When You Were Everything*, and the Flyy Girls Series. Find her on Twitter or Instagram @ashwrites.

April 2022 | Hardcover | $18.99 | 9780358655350 | Houghton Mifflin Harcourt Books for Young Readers

CONVERSATION STARTERS

1. Woodfolk says in the author's note "how ingrained bi-erasure is in our culture." What does she mean by this and what examples in the story illustrate this concept?

2. The story's timeline is told in a non-linear fashion. If Woodfolk had written the story in a more traditional narrative style and with a linear timeline, what effect would it have on the book's message and the relationship between the Narrator and You?

3. Re-read "1232 Days Before the Fire" (39). How does this incident relate to the Narrator's relationship with You? Why does she recount this memory and what do you observe about her emotional strength?

4. What is the symbolic significance of the dilapidated house that the Narrator visits? Does its meaning shift from the first visit to the last?

5. *Nothing Burns as Bright as You* is written in free verse. How does this change the tempo of the storytelling? How does this style help to create a deeper understanding of the Narrator's emotional experience?

6. The use of fire is a key important symbol in the story. It represents the volatility of the relationship between the Narrator and You. Provide other interpretations as fire relates to the central characters and/or supporting characters.

7. A central narrative theme is "the promise of something is better than the actual thing" which is referenced when the Narrator and You are watching movie trailers. Explain the significance of this quote. Do you agree with this idea?

8. *Nothing Burns as Bright as You* is told from the Narrator's point of view. If the story was told from You's point of view, how do you think she would have understood the relationship? Consider her age, socioeconomic, and psychological background. Can you be empathetic to her circumstances?

9. How does the Narrator's relationship with her family help to inform her about her relationship with You? Which family member's advice and wisdom are the most helpful and least? Why?

10. Why do you think Woodfolk wrote the "A Truth" and "A Lie" sections separately and in different formats from each other? How do they play into the overall theme of the story? What do they tell about how the Narrator understands the connection between herself and You?

PASSPORT
Sophia Glock

An unforgettable graphic memoir by debut talent Sophia Glock reveals her discovery as a teenager that her parents are agents working for the CIA

Young Sophia has lived in so many different countries, she can barely keep count. Stationed now with her family in Central America because of her parents' work, Sophia feels displaced as an American living abroad, when she has hardly spent any of her life in America.

Everything changes when she reads a letter she was never meant to see and uncovers her parents' secret. They are not who they say they are. They are working for the CIA. As Sophia tries to make sense of this news, and the web of lies surrounding her, she begins to question everything. The impact that this has on Sophia's emerging sense of self and understanding of the world makes for a page-turning exploration of lies and double lives.

In the hands of this extraordinary graphic storyteller, this astonishing true story bursts to life.

ABOUT THE AUTHOR: **Sophia Glock** is a cartoonist who lives and draws in Austin, Texas. She attended the College of William & Mary and the School of Visual Arts. Her work has been featured in the *New Yorker*, *Buzzfeed*, and *Time Out New York*. She talks to her sister every day.

November 2021 | Hardcover | $24.99 | 9780316458986 |
Little, Brown Books for Young Readers
November 2021 | Paperback | $17.99 | 9780316459006 |
Little, Brown Books for Young Readers

CONVERSATION STARTERS

1. At the beginning of the story, Sophia notes that she hasn't lived anywhere long enough to "be from there" (3). How does the novel discuss the concept of home? How does Sophia's viewpoint on fitting in change over the course of the story?

2. Sophia doesn't want to each lunch alone because, "Nothing will happen" (56). What does that mean? Why does she want "anything" to happen (57)?

3. Why does Sophia want her family to love the play but also wants them to hate it?

4. How does Sophia's family dynamic change when Julia goes to college? When does Sophia start to feel differently about her role within this dynamic?

5. Sophia writes, "What's a lie if everyone gets what they want?" (93). Why does she use this justification? Do you agree with it?

6. Imagine you were assigned Sophia's persuasive essay topic: the literary value of comics. How would you defend your stance? How does the graphic novel format enhance *Passport* as a memoir?

7. Why does Sophia's mother tell her she doesn't have any friends where they live (228)? What does she mean by that?

8. When Sophia's parents tell her their secret, she reacts positively and logically but her father mentions that not all children react well. How do you think you would react? Can you relate to finding out a large secret?

9. Despite her elaborate plans to sneak out of her house while grounded, Sophia decides against it. Why?

10. The novel ends with Sophia starting over again. Sometimes starting over is a good thing, but do you think Sophia feels that way? Why or why not?

11. In the author's note, Sophia says, "Secrets are sticky." What does she mean by that? How is that reflected in the story?

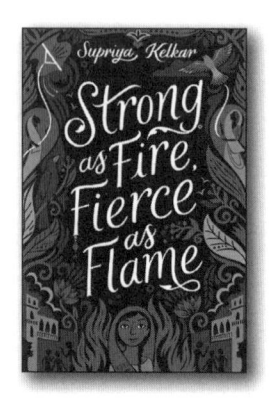

STRONG AS FIRE, FIERCE AS FLAME
Supriya Kelkar

India, 1857

Meera's future has been planned for her for as long as she can remember. As a child, her parents married her to a boy from a neighboring village whom she barely knows. But on the eve of her thirteenth birthday, her husband is killed in the riots following an uprising of Indian soldiers. Meera's father insists that she follow the dictates of their fringe religious sect: end her own life on her husband's funeral pyre.

Risking everything, Meera runs away, escaping into the chaos of the rebellion. But her newfound freedom is short-lived, as she is forced to become a servant in the house of a high-ranking British East India Company captain. Through her work, she gains confidence, new friends, and new skills. But one day, Meera stumbles upon the captain's secret stock of ammunition, destined to be used by the British to continue colonizing India and control its citizens.

Will Meera do her part to take down the British colonists and alert the rebellion of the stockpile? Or will she stay safe and let others make decisions for her? How much fire must a girl face to finally write her own destiny?

"Child marriages, sexist ideologies, and the terrors of colonialism are just a handful of subjects Kelkar scrutinizes through the lens of a teenager in the thick of it. Meera's transformation from a complacent girl to embracing her spirited convictions is nothing short of inspiring." —**Booklist**

"[L]aced with twists, turns, and reveals that are both surprising and riveting ... An absorbing story about a strong girl living during tumultuous times." —*Kirkus Reviews*

ABOUT THE AUTHOR: **Supriya Kelkar** is a screenwriter who has worked on the writing teams for several Hindi films and one Hollywood feature. Her books include *Ahimsa*; *Strong as Fire, Fierce as Flame*; *American as Paneer Pie*; and *That Thing About Bollywood*, among others.

February 2021 | Hardcover | $21.95 | 9781643790404 | Lee & Low Books

CONVERSATION STARTERS

1. The first lines of the book are "My father taught the village boys right outside our little earthen home, but I wasn't a boy, so I didn't get to learn. That didn't stop me from trying, though." What do these lines tell us about how things are in Meera's life? What do they tell us about Meera's character?

2. To "other" someone is to treat or think of a person or a group of people as alien to oneself or one's group. What are some examples of othering in the book?

3. Meera has a very complicated relationship with Memsahib. In what ways does Meera find comfort in Memsahib? How does Meera's thinking change when she realizes what Memsahib really thinks of the South Asian people whose land she is colonizing?

4. Meera cares deeply about the caged koel, Lal, at the Keenes' bungalow. What do you think Meera feels when Lal flies away from his cage? How do you think he has changed her?

5. What are Meera and Bhavani's strengths and weaknesses? How does Meera's friendship with Bhavani challenge her? How does it change her over the course of the story?

6. What do you think the title, "Strong as Fire, Fierce as Flame" means?

7. How does Meera feel about her sister-in-law, Sheela, when she first sees her? How does Meera feel when she first runs into Sheela at the market in Indranagar? How is that different from Meera's interaction with Sheela the next time they meet at the market?

8. What does Ravi's kite mean to Meera? How do you think she feels when she flies it?

9. What does the word "decolonize" mean to you?

10. Why do you think the author chose to include such a detailed historical note at the end of the book?

11. Look at the cover. What symbolism do you see there?

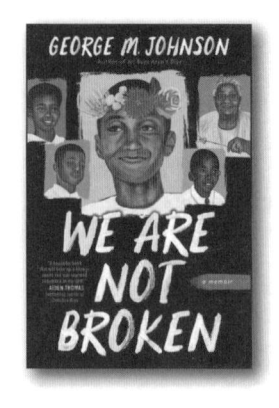

WE ARE NOT BROKEN
George M. Johnson

George M. Johnson, activist and bestselling author of *All Boys Aren't Blue*, returns with a striking memoir that celebrates Black boyhood and brotherhood in all its glory.

This is the vibrant story of George, Garrett, Rall, and Rasul — four children raised by Nanny, their fiercely devoted grandmother. The boys hold one another close through early brushes with racism, memorable experiences at the family barbershop, and first loves and losses. And with Nanny at their center, they are never broken.

George M. Johnson captures the unique experience of growing up as a Black boy in America, and their rich family stories — exploring themes of vulnerability, sacrifice, and culture — are interspersed with touching letters from the grandchildren to their beloved matriarch. By turns heartwarming and heartbreaking, this personal account is destined to become a modern classic of emerging adulthood.

"Deeply impactful. George M. Johnson has done it again!" —**Nic Stone**, *New York Times* **bestselling author of** *Dear Martin*

"This is lush luxurious art doing hard messy heartwork." —**Kiese Laymon**, **award-winning author of** *Long Division*

"Intimate. Revelatory. Powerful. A must-read journey" —**Mark Oshiro**, **award-winning author of** *Anger is a Gift*

"Love—deep, soulful, clarifying love—shines in George M. Johnson's writing." —**Saeed Jones, award-winning author of** *How We Fight For Our Lives*

"Striking and joyful. This book is love!" —**Laurie Halse Anderson**, *New York Times* **bestselling author of** *Shout*

ABOUT THE AUTHOR: **George M. Johnson** is an award winning Black non-binary writer, author, and activist based in the New York City area and the author of memoirs *We Are Not Broken* and *All Boys Aren't Blue*. They have written on race, gender, sex, and culture for *Essence*, *The Advocate*, BuzzFeed News, *Teen Vogue*, and more than forty other national publications.

September 2021 | Hardcover | $17.99 | 9780759554603 |
Little, Brown Books for Young Readers

CONVERSATION STARTERS

1. *We Are Not Broken* opens with the Malcolm X quote: "The most disrespected person in America is the Black woman." How do the women in George's life support and care for them and their brothers? How, in turn, do George and their brothers uplift the Black women in their lives?

2. Each chapter is titled after a Nannyism, one of George's grandmother's pearls of wisdom. Which of these sayings resonated with you the most? Why? What sayings have been passed down through your own family?

3. Garrett, Rall, George, and Rasul consider themselves brothers. How is this closeness reflected in their family dynamic? What makes these cousins as close as brothers?

4. How does everyone in George's family benefit from intergenerational relationships? How do members of the different generations care for one another? How do these relationships change over time?

5. Why is childhood important? In what ways does society force Black children to grow up too soon?

6. Throughout this book and *All Boys Aren't Blue*, George talks about the way boys are taught to behave. How does that gendered conditioning impact George's navigation of their gender identity? How do models of "traditional" masculinity affect young boys?

7. What does each boy's letter to Nanny reveal about their individual relationship with her? Did you respond strongly to one letter in particular? Why?

8. What role do faith and spirituality play in George's life? In Nanny's? How are their relationships with religion shaped by their identities?

9. Nanny is a singular presence in the lives of these four boys. What do you learn about Nanny through her relationships with her grandchildren? How does she exert her role as matriarch?

10. George repeatedly singles out the importance of Black joy. How is joy expressed in each of these stories? Why is joy so important to celebrate?

BOOK GROUP FAVORITES FROM 2020

We asked thousands of book groups to tell us what books they read and discussed during 2019 that they enjoyed most. The top titles were:

FICTION

The Book Woman of Troublesome Creek
Kim Michele Richardson
Sourcebooks

The Flight Attendant
Chris Bohjalian | Vintage

Circe
Madeline Miller
Little, Brown & Co

The Only Woman in the Room
Marie Benedict | Sourcebooks

A Good Neighborhood
Therese Anne Fowler | St Martin's

The Orphan Collector
Ellen Marie Wiseman | Kensington

Normal People
Sally Rooney | Hogarth

The Red Address Book
Sofia Lundberg | HMH

The Guest Book
Sarah Blake | Flatiron Books

Washington Black
Esi Edugyan | Vintage

Midnight at the Blackbird Cafe
Heather Webber | Forge Books

NONFICTION

999
Heather Dune Macadam
Kensington Books

Becoming
Michelle Obama | Crown

Yale Needs Women
Anne Gardiner Perkins
Sourcebooks

Lab Girl
Hope Jahren | Vintage

Motherhood So White
Nefertiti Austin | Sourcebooks

The Hello Girls
Elizabeth Cobbs
Harvard University Press — TIE

Things We Didn't Talk About When I Was a Girl
Jeannie Vanasco
Tin House Books

Goodbye My Havana
Anna Veltfort | Redwood Press

Here We Are
Aarti Namdev Shahani | Celadon

High Achiever
Tiffany Jenkins | Harmony

YOUNG ADULT

I'm Not Dying With You Tonight
Kimberly Jones & Gilly Segal
Sourcebooks Fire

We Are Here to Stay
Susan Kuklin | Candlewickl

Merci Suárez Changes Gears
Meg Medina | Candlewick — TIE

The Hate U Give
Angie Thomas | Balzer + Bray

The Fountains of Silence
Ruta Sepetys | Philomel Books

Becoming Beatriz
Tami Charles | Charlesbridge

The Next Great Paulie Fink
Ali Benjamin | LBYR

In the Neighborhood of True
Susan Kaplan Carlton | AYR

The Assassination of Brangwain Spurge
M.T. Anderson | Candlewick

Please visit ReadingGroupChoices.com between January 1 and April 1, 2022 to enter our 2021 Favorite Books Contest by telling us about your favorite books of 2021. You will be entered for a chance to win bookstore gift certificates to use toward your meetings plus books for each person in your group, compliments of our publishing partners.

READING GROUP CHOICES

Selections for Lively Discussions

GUIDELINES FOR LIVELY BOOK DISCUSSIONS

1. RESPECT SPACE - Avoid "crosstalk" or talking over others.
2. ALLOW SPACE - Some of us are more outgoing and others more reserved. If you've had a chance to talk, allow others time to offer their thoughts as well.
3. BE OPEN - Keep an open mind, learn from others, and acknowlege there are differences in opinon. That's what makes it interesting!
4. OFFER NEW THOUGHTS - Try not to repeat what others have said, but offer a new perspective.
5. STAY ON THE TOPIC - Contribute to the flow of conversation by holding your comments to the topic of the book, keeping personal references to an appropriate medium.

Great Books ∽ Great People ∽ Great Conversation

DO YOU LOVE TO READ?

Spread the joy of reading and build a sense of community by starting a Little Free Library book exchange!

Hailed by the *New York Times* as "a global sensation", Little Free Library book exchanges are "take a book, return a book" gathering places where neighbors share their favorite literature and stories.

LITTLE FREE LIBRARY.ORG
TAKE A BOOK • RETURN A BOOK

Find locations near you and learn how to start your own at *www.littlefreelibrary.org*

INTRODUCING THE NEXT GREAT AUTHOR

Indies Introduce.
It's what independent booksellers have been doing forever – discovering and championing new authors.

INDIES
Introduce

See titles at
BookWeb.org/indiesintroduce

READING GROUP CHOICES

READING GROUP CHOICES' ADVISORY BOARD

Charlie Mead owned and managed Reading Group Choices from 2005 until 2014. He sold the business to Mary Morgan in April 2014. Charlie's business partner and wife, Barbara Drummond Mead, co-owned and managed the business until her passing in 2011. From 1972 to 1999, Charlie served at Digital Equipment Corporation (DEC) and Compaq Computer Corporation, both now part of Hewlett Packard, most recently as vice president of communication accounts worldwide. In 1999, Charlie became vice president of Sales of Interpath Communications Corporation, an Internet infrastructure company, until the company's sale in 2000. From 2000 to 2005, Charlie owned and managed Connxsys LLC, a communications consulting firm.

Donna Paz Kaufman founded Reading Group Choices in 1994 to connect publishers, booksellers, libraries, and readers with great books for group discussion. Today, Paz & Associates owns Story & Song Bookstore Bistro and continues to assist people around the globe open, manage, and sell their independent bookstores in The Bookstore Training Group. To learn more about Paz & Associates, visit PazBookBiz.com.

John Mutter is editor-in-chief of *Shelf Awareness*, the daily e-mail newsletter focusing on books, media about books, retailing and related issues to help booksellers, librarians and others do their jobs more effectively. Before he and his business partner, Jenn Risko, founded the company in May 2005, he was executive editor of bookselling at *Publishers Weekly*. He has covered book industry issues for 25 years and written for a variety of publications, including *The Bookseller* in the U.K.; *Australian Bookseller & Publisher*; *Boersenblatt*, the German book trade magazine; and *College Store Magazine* in the U.S. For more information about *Shelf Awareness*, go to its website, shelf-awareness.com.

Megan Hanson's background includes extensive customer service work, experience coordinating marketing campaigns for the Madrid-based NGO Colegas, plus serving as a Community Literacy Coordinator for the Madison non-profit Literacy Network. Since 2012, she has been working for the internationally-recognized non-profit Little Free Library, helping them to develop and scale to meet demand. Her focus is on digital marketing, data and web management, product development and customer service.

René Martin is the Events Director/Publicist at Quail Ridge Books in Raleigh, NC. "Nancy Olson, who owned and operated Quail Ridge Books & Music from 1981 until it was sold in 2013, hired me in 2000. I knew nothing about the book business, but said yes, it would be fun. And it has been! Sixteen years later I now know a little more about the book business, and love being the events coordinator/publicist for Quail Ridge Books. We now host almost 300 events a year. My goal is to make QRB a model publicity department, and we have a beautiful, new store in which to make that happen."

Nicole Sullivan opened BookBar, a community bookstore wine bar in 2013. Immediately recognizing a need to connect readers with book clubs in their area, she then founded bookclubhub.org in 2014. BookBed, an author bed & breakfast located just above the book store opened its doors in Fall of 2015. Additionally, she has funneled her passion for helping others to create successful bookstore / bar & cafe models through her work as a consultant with Paz & Associates. Nicole proudly serves as co-President and founder of her neighborhood business association, Tennyson Berkeley Business Association (TBBA) and as Treasurer of her local maintenance district for the city of Denver.

READING GROUP CHOICES ANNUAL GUIDES

Fiction, nonfiction, and young adult book recommendations are included in each annual edition.

Order online at www.ReadingGroupChoices.com

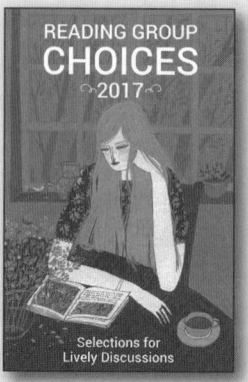